HEROES

A psychological insight into men's perceptions on relationships

Micki Pistorius

Author's note:

Whenever I testify as an expert witness psychologist in court, I always make a point of declaring: I am not here to condemn or condone the behaviour, but to explain the behaviour. The same principle applies to this book.

I am not saying what men do is fair from a woman's point of view. I am telling it as it is, as the men have related it to me. Men and women think differently. Not only do men think differently about relationships than women, they think differently than women think men think. Think about that. I am also not writing this book to teach women how to catch men. If a woman tries to catch a man, she has already lost him. If women want to adapt their behaviour and get in touch with their own femininity, which may just happen to appeal to the heroes out there, then so be it. If women prefer to be pugnacious and hell-bent on cutting men down to size, it is their choice. Men don't find it very appealing. If men read this book and feel the need to up their game and man-up: good, because the human race needs heroes.

Dedicated to Odysseus.

Prologue

I have walked with heroes and hunted villains. No one needs to remind me of how bad men can be. Perhaps my proficiency in profiling the very worst of men many years ago, also cultivated my ability to recognise good men – the heroes. This book is inspired by the everyday, unsung heroes who have crossed my path.

Men are born with the innate instinct to provide and protect. It is what makes them men, it defines their "raison d'être" on earth. Intrinsically they know, if they align their existence with this dual purpose, then they are good men, heroes. The ratio of providing and protecting may fluctuate in different men. Some may be 80 percent protector and 20 percent provider, like policemen, who unfortunately do not earn enough to support their families. Some men are better providers than protectors. Not all men are macho heroes. Some aim for a 50-50 providing and protecting ratio. Whatever that ratio, it remains the benchmark of the hero thing. Exceptionally few have no families to provide for or to protect, but their strength of character and generosity become a legacy that benefits all mankind. This is when a hero becomes a legend.

What disturbs the hero's mental equilibrium most is being the anti-hero. They detest it and they will try to avoid it at all costs. I remember years ago when I was still a profiler, the murder and robbery detectives used to enjoy a barbeque on a Friday afternoon. This social institution was not restricted to men. Some of these detectives were women, and myself obviously also being a woman, we joined our male colleagues. At about 4pm we would prepare to go home. At this time their cell phones usually began to ring; the wives calling their husbands to remind them to pick up bread and milk on their way home. The wives would then hear the voices of the female colleagues in the background and scold the men for "having a good time with the girls". Many a time I watched the men unpack everything, buying more drink and cavorting till the early hours of the morning. Men resent being falsely accused of being the anti-hero. Some men reason that if they are being falsely accused of being the anti-hero, they might as well live up to that expectation.

CONTENTS

ACTION HEROES:
PROTECTORS AND WARRIORS

Men don't talk. They do

When we buy a doll for a girl, we buy her a Barbie doll. When we buy a "doll" for a boy, we buy him an action hero – a Superman. The word "action" is very important. I often advise women not to pay too much attention to what a man says, for he may often promise her the world, and he may even believe it at that moment, but what is more important, are his sustained actions. Men are action orientated.

Men express themselves mainly through their actions. If he loves a woman, he will solve her problems, he will gratify her needs and wishes, he will buy her things, he will fix her life, and he will work hard to provide for her. He will set out to make her happy.

Despite them being action orientated, when I ask men what the most important element of a relationship is, they do not unanimously answer: "Sex". They do unanimously answer: "Communication." Now this is interesting. Does this mean the doers want to talk? Sometimes they do want to talk, especially if they trust a woman. And then the woman perpetually interrupts him, or she does not listen to him.

Listen

When a woman listens to a man when he tells her something, without interrupting him, he gets the message that he is important to her and that she is paying attention. If she interrupts, he feels unimportant. Sometimes it is a good idea not to respond immediately. She could rather ponder on what he had said and come back to him a few days later with a suggestion or a response, instead of offering him immediate advice. To a man, immediate advice sounds as if she is disagreeing with him. "I have been thinking about what you discussed with me yesterday. I wondered if ... what do you think?" Just by adjusting her mode of communication, she circumvents sounding as if she is criticising. Of course she is entitled to a different opinion, as long as it does not make him sound stupid.

> **Case example:** A woman asked her husband why he doesn't invite me as a motivational speaker at his company. He answered: "We have already booked a speaker for this term." "But you can always change it. I think it is a good idea to ask her," she continued. She repeated herself three times. Clearly, she did not hear him. He said No, three times. She was embarrassing him by insisting. Also she was telling him what to do at his place of work. (Then she wondered why he slammed the car door!) Some women tend to think if they just keep on repeating themselves, they may actually convince the men of their good idea. Or she thinks if he does not immediately agree with her, he did not hear her in the first place. He heard her. He said No. Did she hear him?

"Sometimes a good communicator is a person who just knows when to shut up," said one man. Another man said: "It takes much courage for a man to open himself up. Don't later use what he told you against him as a vicious backlash."

Truly listening to someone does not imply merely keeping quiet when someone else is talking. It entails a cognitive effort to interpret the essence of the message the other person is communicating, seeing the message from that person's perspective, attempting to understand that person's underlying emotions and motivations, foreseeing how that person will act on the message and only once these cognitive actions have been completed can the listener then consider what is his/her response, emotions and the probable impact that the response will have on the other person. Listening is a complicated cognitive ACTION, not just a passive waiting for a breather to jump in.

Needs vs. needy

A man wants a woman to communicate her needs to him. How else would he be able to fulfil her needs, if he does not know what she wants? He cannot read her mind, so she has to tell him. However, it often happens, once she communicates her needs, he calls her "needy". So, I ask the men, what is the difference between a woman communicating her needs and a needy woman? A man wants a woman to need him, but he does not want her to be helpless and her needs must not distract him too much from his quest and require his full-time attention. It is fine for her to communicate her needs, but it depends how she does it and if she is persistent, she is needy. Timing is very important too – if it interferes with something else, he would rather do, she is needy. If she shows appreciation, he is likely to continue fulfilling her needs, if she criticises, she is needy.

One man explained: "Like women, men need me-time too. When she clings to you like a heart-lung machine, she is needy. When I speak to another woman and she suddenly grabs my arm, interrupts and kisses my face, it is embarrassing, and she is very needy." One man gave me a very clear and precise answer – the difference between having needs and being needy is: "Nagging."

Regarding timing, one man commented: "If she tells me she needs it done immediately and I drop whatever I planned doing, to do it for her, and I later discover it was not that urgent at all, then next time she requires me to do something urgently, I will disregard her ideas of how and when things need to be done. If she tells me why she needs it, I can determine how urgent it is."

If he feels needed and he can do something for her, which she cannot do by herself, then he feels good about himself as a man. One man also explained: "If what she requires of me involves a heroic deed, I will do it, but I am also not just her puppy at her beck and call just because she wants me to hang around. Then she is needy. I have stuff to do." Warriors have dragons to fight.

> **Case example:** A man liked a certain woman, but dreaded visiting her, because he knew that would entail them sitting on the couch and talking. He was an introvert and shy and the thought of having nothing to say to her caused him much anxiety. Eventually he plucked up the courage and rang her doorbell. It was out of order. He called her and she opened the door. "Bring me a screwdriver," he said, "so I can fix this doorbell." She did. "Since I am busy fixing this, do you have anything else that needs repairing?" he asked. She did. He spent the whole afternoon adjusting the geysers, changing light bulbs, fixing hair dryers, backwashing the pool pump and all the other bothersome little odd jobs. She brought him coffee while he was working and they chatted. She also thanked him every time for repairing and adjusting everything and she smiled a lot. He later told me he had never had such a great time getting to know a girl. He was the action man, DOING stuff for her, and she was appreciative, TELLING him how great he is. Perfect

 Read more about: INTROVERTS and EXTROVERTS on page 156

Stop telling them what to do

Women talk, men do. Many women, unfortunately, have this astounding idea that they can and should tell men what to do. Men are men. They are strong warriors and they know what to do. They resent it when a woman tells them what to do. Several things happen when a woman tells a man to do something. Firstly, she is communicating to him that she is trying to control his life. When we try to control someone, it is a vote of no confidence in their own capabilities. He is the hero – he is in charge of his life. Secondly, telling is a top-down communication. It is a command. The woman is not the man's commander. Trust him. Don't tell him. One man told me: "Women talk to men as if they are boys. If I don't know how to do something, I will figure it out." Or he will read the manual while on the toilet.

> **Case example:** A woman was dating a father of a baby daughter. She told him over the phone: "Leave the baby with your Mom for the night and drive over to my place. I never see you." He did not. He did not even answer his phone for the rest of the weekend. (I can already see all the men nodding their heads.) She was telling him what to do, giving him instructions. And she was criticising him. And she was being demanding. And she was trying to control him. If she had said: "I am missing you and would like to see you. Is it possible for your Mom to babysit and can you visit me? It would make me happy," he would have made a plan.

Communicating a need does not imply using that TONE OF VOICE and ordering him about.

> **Case example:** It was early evening. The wife was busy tending to the baby. "You make dinner," she said to the husband who had just arrived home. She did not ask nicely, but he just nodded and proceeded to take the meat from the fridge. "You have to defrost it first and then cook it ..." she continued. He prepared the food silently and went to bed early. Don't ask a man to do something and then tell him how to do it.

Don't help a man. He is an action hero. He can do it himself

Some women do not tell men what to do, but they do help men. Women are by nature very helpful creatures. For example, when a woman in a queue at a check-out counter, tells the woman behind her, she forgot an item and dashes off to fetch it, the one behind will push the absent woman's trolley for her. Generally, men won't push another man's trolley. To women it is sociable to help. To men it is a sign of weakness. Never help a man. Unless he asks, which he seldom will, and then don't make a fuss about it. A woman should not offer to help a man paint the chairs. She can ask if she can join him. He may ask her to help him change the tyre and to pass him the thingamajig. She should not tell him how her Dad had taught her to change the tyre and that he is doing it all wrong. If he is struggling to unlock the front door, she should not take the key out of his hand, not even if he is a bit tipsy. Does she just have to stand there and wait patiently until he gets it right? Yes, and then she smiles and thanks him. I did not say it is fair.

One man explained it as follows: "Core to a woman's essence is her appearance. Therefore, a man should not tell her to go on a diet because she is fat. Core to a man's essence is his competence. Therefore, a woman should not tell him to get a professional, because he is useless at fixing things. If she goes on a diet of her own accord, then he can support her, and if he gets a professional of his own accord, then she can thank him."

> **Case example:** The woman arrives home with a car full of groceries. He comes out and asks or tells her he will carry the grocery bags in for her. Naturally she picks up a few bags... Don't touch the bags! She is conveying the message to him that he is not strong enough to do this simple task for her. The same goes for luggage. She can enter the house and start unpacking the groceries. She can also pop open a can of beer for him when he's done. (All the men agreed unanimously on this one.) What does she do when one of those bags tear and the tin cans roll down the driveway? She looks the other way and pretends she did not see. Anyway, she is supposed to be in the kitchen unpacking the groceries, not in the driveway. She can laugh with him about it later, but only when he already has the beer in his hand.

Helping and supporting has a different meaning to men and women

> **Case example:** An unemployed engineer complained to me that he wished his girlfriend would support him. His girlfriend on the other hand told me she supported him, but he refused to co-operate. I realised here was a communication problem. She told me she supported him

14

in the following manner: "When I get home at night after a long day's work, I tell him, come sit by me and I will update your CV on the computer. Then he just gives me a look and resumes watching television. Also, I bought all the engineering magazines and cut out all the ads looking for engineers and I told him to follow them up." Usually when I read this verbatim quote to men, they cringe. She is telling him what to do, she is doing it for him. That is not helping or supporting him. That is a vote of no confidence. I asked the man how he would like her to support him. He answered: "She can just tell me she believes in me. She can tell me I am only going through a bad patch, but things will pick up and I am the best engineer in the world. That will inspire me." Women talk, men do. Generally, if women tell men how great they are, then they inspire the men into action.

One man explained: "Men do not want to be seen as failures. Being unemployed is a major failure. If she can just assure him that she is there, that she will not leave him and that he is not alone in that mess, then she is supportive."

Men want to resolve women's problems. When she tells him about something, he feels obliged to fix it for her. He wants to be the hero and help her. For example, she tells him about some problem she had at work with a co-worker. He interrupts and wants to know what the outcome was. He needs to determine how he can fix it. He is often surprised that she has already fixed it. "Then why tell me about it?" he asks. Because she wants to TELL you about it. Women talk, get it! A man will never tell another man: "I had a flat tyre today and I changed it." A woman will.

One of my clients has the following agreement with his wife. When she wants to tell him about something he asks: "Is this an issue you want me to do something about, or can I just sit and scratch my butt while listening?" So determine if it is a problem, or just a butt scratcher. If it is only a butt scratcher, the man just needs to sit and listen and make the appropriate noises. "And what are the appropriate noises?" ask the men. Just say: "And what did you say... and what did she say... and what did you say..." and pay attention to her. You would want her to pay attention to you when you tell her something.

When he can't fix it

A man wants to tend to a woman's problems. Fixing a problem is a heroic action. However, when he cannot fix the problem for some reason, he has one of two reactions. He will either attack her or ignore her.

> **Case example:** A woman is crying because her dog died. The man says: "Stop crying!" And he goes and buys her another puppy. Or he ignores her, gets in his car and drives off and she thinks: "You heartless idiot." And he returns with a puppy. In both cases the man can't understand why she did not want the puppy? Men are very pragmatic. He fixed the problem by replacing the puppy. Actually he would do anything to make her stop crying. Men are clueless about what to do when a woman cries, because they don't know how to fix the problem. (Here is a tip guys: When she cries, just hold her. Don't say anything. Just hold her. That's it.) If women can only understand that his strange or boorish actions are due to his frustrations, because if he can't fix her problem he is the anti-hero. And he hates being the anti-hero. So he walks away and ignores her, or worse, he yells at her. And women have to understand this about men. I did not say it is fair. It's just the way it is.

A colleague of mine explained men are empathic on a cognitive level, as opposed to women who are empathic on an emotional level. Men need to separate themselves from the emotional content in order to make objective decisions to solve the problem. On an intellectual level they understand the emotion, but they cannot allow themselves to be submerged in the emotion, for then they would not be able to take rational action. Men are action orientated, remember.

Sometimes he does try to hug her and just hold her and then she pushes him away. He is trying. Acknowledge it.

There are times however, guys, when women really need you to step up. When your wife calls you in tears because she just had a car accident, it is not the time to attack her, or ignore her. Bite your tongue.

If a woman criticises everything a man does and if she does everything

16

herself, he feels useless and inadequate. It is a recipe for disaster. Unfortunately, it originates in childhood with mothers doing everything for their sons, and continuously criticising their boys. Fathers usually get upset when mothers do too much for the boys, for it is in a man's nature TO BE ACTIVE and to figure it out for himself. Praising him for figuring it out will boost his self-esteem. Doing it for him or criticising him conveys the message that he is incompetent. How would he be able to fix adult problems and fight dragons if he is not taught to figure it out for himself as a young boy. Denying him this natural growth opportunity and being over-protective is actually psychological castration. At about the age of six, boys need to identify with a father figure and get involved in male activities, without a mother hovering about trying to protect them from the father figure. (This was the age when young boys were taken away from their Spartan mothers and turned into warriors.)

I have encountered many grown men who have terrible adult relationships with their mothers, because they resent the mothers' smothering them as children. As adult men they often punish their mothers in various ways, usually by avoiding them and cutting them out of their adult lives, in an attempt to get even for childhood wounds incurred. This act in itself makes them feel as anti-heroes, which exacerbates the situation. They often also have exaggerated over-reactions when any woman engages in a nurturing action that reminds them of their mothers – even just packing them a lunch box or reminding them to take their vitamins. Telling him to take his vitamins, is acting like his mother. Just leaving vitamins out for him to take, without verbally reminding him, is supportive and showing you care about his health.

Some women can be very, very bossy. Sometimes I wonder if some of them are born that way.

> **Case example**: A man married a widow with three young daughters. He moved into their home. One morning he let the dogs into the kitchen. The cute little 7 year old in her pink pyjamas promptly pointed her finger at him, wagged it up and down and in THAT tone of voice said: "Uncle John, in this house, we don't let the dogs in. Don't let me catch you doing it again." Men do not like it if anybody

points fingers at them, not even cute little 7 year olds in pink pyjamas.

Never ask "Why"

Another fatal mistake women make when communicating with men is to ask "why." To a man "why" translates to: "You don't know what you are doing, you incompetent stupid fool." All men, without exception agree on this one.

> **Case example:** A husband and his wife travel in the car. She innocently asks him: "Lovey, why are you driving this route?" What he hears is: "Listen you stupid dumb fool, you don't know where you are going." Believe me when I tell this story, all the men burst out laughing and then agree that is exactly what they hear. If his buddy had asked the same question he would have answered: "Because I heard on the radio there are road works on the usual road." But because the "why" came from his wife or girlfriend, he regards it as a vote of no confidence. He is her hero at all times and he is in control of the situation. There should be no reason for her to doubt him. The same applies to "Why don't you tell your boss...." "Why don't you use the star screwdriver..." DELETE THE WORD WHY.

I asked the men what would be an acceptable rephrase of "why" and the following suggestions came up: "This is interesting. How come..." or "I don't understand how ..." or "You have probably thought about this, but maybe it's a good idea to ..."

Do not say: "Can you explain to me..." because that sounds like his mother or teacher. If the woman approaches the issue in one of these alternative ways and he just stares at her, it means he heard her, and he thinks her suggestion is a very good idea. Does she really expect him to verbalise that it is a good idea? For Pete's sake, he is a man. Then he goes off and he does it the way she suggested. Then she should not tell him: "I told you so." She should just tell him how great he is and that he is her hero. And mean it. He knows.

18

The typical vote of no confidence

Speaking about cars. This is a potentially disastrous area. Women are prone to tell a man how he should drive! A man is a strong capable warrior in charge of a heavy dangerous, complicated, expensive machine and he has her life in his trust. And then she tells him what to do? The woman should not doubt his ability to handle this machine. She should rather sit back, relax and look out of the window if looking ahead makes her nervous. If he gets lost, so what. Don't say anything. He knows. What is more important? Her relationship with this man or the first 15 minutes of a movie that she may be missing? Men usually only start driving recklessly when women complain about their driving. It is a knee-jerk reaction. Maybe she can pre-empt the situation with a comment like: "I get nervous in a car, but I know you will take it gently and look after me." Anyway guys, you are supposed to protect her, so man-up and make her feel safe, rather than driving like a jerk to scare her. The pay-off of feeling like a hero by keeping her safe, is much greater than feeling like an ass who tried to show-off. (Tip to the men: Driving recklessly may impress other males, but it only scares a woman and if you scare her, she is certainly not going to sleep with you! Get it?)

Men are exceptionally sensitive to criticism and often experience even seemingly innocent comments as a vote of no confidence. And yes, it has to do with their egos. I have no problem with men's egos. They need egos, they are warriors. They defend us. Without egos they are not men. If a woman cannot deal with a man's ego, she should date a woman. I do also agree that some egos are vastly inflated, but we will discuss that later.

Women pre-navigate dialogue

> **Case example:** A husband needed to confront a relative about a problem and he had been postponing this event. Eventually his wife became clearly impatient and insisted that he takes action. "But what must I do?" asked the husband. Whereupon the wife just got up and walked off. The husband was baffled. "Do?" she replied when she had calmed down. "You must get in your car and drive over there and talk to them. That is the action that is required.

How can you ask me what you must do?" What the husband meant was: "What must I say to them?" Women talk, men do.

Women have an amazing ability to pre-navigate a complete dialogue in their heads, the same way a man would navigate a forthcoming road trip in his mind. "If he says this, then I say that and if he says this, then I will say so," etc. Eventually the woman will map the conversation to reach the specific outcome she desires. Armed with this verbal map, she engages in a discussion or argument. No wonder men avoid verbal conflicts with women. However, if a man can only recognise this ability in his female partner as a resource, imagine what a useful tool it could be for him when he has to confront other people. It is a pity that men do not want to ask: "What should I say?"

Like a yin and yang symbol that forms a perfect circle, half black, half white, if men and women can only grasp that their differences can complement each other, instead of perceiving the differences as threats. If we were all the same, it would be a mishmash of greys. (And I am not speaking of Shades of Grey – that is another book.) Strengths and weaknesses can complement each other. Mostly women offer advice or suggest alternatives, not because they criticise the men, but because they are on his team, they do have his back, they have the intelligence to make a meaningful contribution and this is her way of supporting him. If only he can step outside his ego for a second and give her the benefit of the doubt. Even generals consult and consider suggestions.

Men do rate communication as an important element of a relationship, but they underestimate the vital importance thereof.

> **Case example:** A man asked his wife to proof-read his presentation to the company's board meeting. She was a linguist and corrected his grammar. "You can't say it like this, it's wrong," she said. "Are you saying I don't know how to do my work?" he yelled. She threw the document in the corner and stormed out of the room. "You disappoint me," she screamed. "He attacked me, when I was only trying to help him. Why did he ask me, if he did not want my advice?" she asked me later. I explained to her that her hurt feelings were valid, but that he

experienced her comment as criticism, because she told him he was wrong. Had she worded it differently, he would have accepted her correction. I explained to him that he could have regarded her linguistic training as an allied resource in his camp, rather than an attack from an enemy. By yelling at her and hurting her feelings, he alienated her. He also did not stick to the subject. The subject was the grammar, not his capacity to do his work. This was a typical example of miscommunication.

Case example: A man told me he spends much time at work making lists of all the handyman tasks he plans on doing at home. I asked him if he had told his wife about this list. "No," he said, "do you think I should?" So, we have the wife at home. Living with all the little handyman jobs that need to be done, wondering if he is ever going to get to them, but she does not want to complain or nag, so she becomes quiet and sulking and sour faced. He avoids going home because she is quiet and sulking and sour faced and that is why the handyman jobs never get done. If only he told her he is making a list, she would flip over backwards just to know he is thinking about it, and about her, at work. He just never thought of telling her. Did she remember to tell him how grateful she is that he is doing this for her? It works both ways.

One man said the difference between whining and nagging is: whining is when she is complaining and there is no hope of a solution, nagging is when she makes the issue his problem.

Men catch balls, not hints

Case example: The wife says: "Wow, the grass is growing wild," or "it looks like a jungle out there." He looks outside and says: "Yeah." He wonders why she is stating something obvious. Come Saturday, she says: "I asked you so nicely to mow the lawn and now the guests are coming over and just look at it." He answers: "No you did not." He is right. She did not ask him to mow the lawn. She said the grass was growing wild. Had she said: "Would you please mow the lawn before Saturday because your parents are coming over for lunch," he would have known exactly what she wanted and why she wanted it and when she wanted it done by. Come Saturday morning, she should rather not say: "Remember you promised to mow the lawn." It sounds like criticism. Men prefer feedback. A friendly reminder like: "I'm so glad you are going to mow the lawn, while I prepare lunch for your parents," would do. Once he has mowed the lawn and she gives him a beer, she can ask him to clean the patio, but she needs to be specific, because it looks clean to him. "Please unpack the plastic chairs, they are too heavy for me and would you mind wiping them with a cloth, they are dusty and women don't like sitting on dirty chairs." (Guys don't mind dirty chairs. Women wear floral dresses or white jeans.) So he takes a wet cloth and he smears the dust. Don't say anything. Now she can ask him to go to the shops and buy charcoal and three lemons for his favourite lemon meringue pie. While he is gone she can quickly wash the muddy white plastic chairs. When he returns from running the errand, she thanks him and invites him to join her in the shower before his parents arrive. He is very happy, he could be the hero and do stuff for her, and he is getting a joint shower and who knows what may happen then. And he is getting lemon meringue pie.

Don't tell him, touch him. It is an action he understands

Case example: A young woman was very much in love with a man. No matter how much she flirted with him, he just did not get it. I asked the other men for advice to help the young woman. What should a woman do to convey to a man that she likes him? They all unanimously responded: "Touch him." Later the young woman brought her boyfriend so I could meet him. "Did you never realise she was flirting with you?" I asked. "No," he replied. "I thought she was flirting with my friend. I could not

believe a girl like her would be remotely interested in me."
"When did you realise it was you?" I asked. "She came up to me one day and placed her one little hand on my shoulder and held her other wrist under my nose and asked me to smell her new perfume. I melted and could literally feel my legs buckle." He actually blushed when he told me.

Oxytocin is a neurotransmitter released by the brain and is commonly called the "cuddle hormone". Women produce much more oxytocin than men, but interestingly enough, when men inhale oxytocin by nasal spray it improves their ability to interpret emotional and mental states of other people. Now women do not need to inject inhalers in men's noses when they sleep to improve their emotional intelligence. The good news is that a good hug can cause an oxytocin release. So does sex. A well-known neuropsychologist reports that men need to be touched two or three times more frequently than women to maintain the same level of oxytocin. Oxytocin also happens to be a good antidote to the stress hormone cortisol. So, if women want men to be more empathic to their emotions, then women should touch men more often. Nothing beats scratching his back ... almost nothing.

Arguing with men is futile

Men are by nature an aggressive species. They have to be, how else would they protect us? As in days of yore, modern man's daily life still consists of real and metaphorical battlefields. His neurological wiring has remained the same for millennia. The moment he encounters another human, he decides within 15 milliseconds if this is a friend or an enemy, based upon the other person's tone of voice and facial expressions. This is a pre-conscious neurological action. If he recognises an enemy his brain sends messages within 100 milliseconds to his torso, preparing his body for battle, before he is actually consciously aware of it. If you are an enemy, it is game on!

When anybody, including a woman, engages on a hostile level with a man, his aggression escalates. As soon as men are challenged with aggression, then their own aggression becomes justified to them. Once swords are drawn on the battlefield, he automatically goes into warrior mode. Pretty soon we have two people yelling at each other, or worse, physically attacking each other. In any case what makes us think that any person is going to be willing and inclined to give us what we want, when we yell at them? Just where is the logic in that? Men may also just retreat into their camp in an attempt to disengage from the fight, because fighting with a woman is anti-hero behaviour.

Think about it. Mostly we get angry at another person when that person does not want to do what we want him or her to do, or we get angry when someone else tells us to do something we don't want to do. What makes us think that we have the right, power, authority or audacity to tell another adult what they must do?

We all have a right and responsibility to admonish someone not to break the law. We should all know the law. We all also have the right to state our individual boundaries of what we regard as acceptable or unacceptable behaviour. If someone else persists in non-compliance, and in abusing our boundaries, we can leave. Walk away. Do not share your time or space with someone who does not respect you, but do not assume it is acceptable to expect another person, or your partner, to do everything exactly as you want them to. (Unless you are paying them in an employment situation.) If everybody thought the same way you do, then the Creator would have created only one prototype and there would be billions of other cloned YOUs on earth and no diversity. People differ from each other. It is not right or wrong. It is just different. If you cannot live with the difference, it is acceptable to leave, but violence and force and manipulation are not conducive to a relationship.

A woman does not have to fight or manipulate a man to do what she wants him to do

> **Case example**: A husband returned home at 2am, after a night out with the boys. He was expecting a confrontation. Men are not stupid. They know when they are in trouble. The wife, in bed, was clearly sleeping. (Note, she did not stay up and wait for him.) Instead of yelling at him when he stumbled into the bedroom, she greeted him normally - not with a smile, but definitely not with the icy voice. "Hi, I'm glad you're home safe. Let's go to sleep." He attempted to make an excuse or defend himself, because he was expecting the fight. She just repeated: "It's late, let's go to

24

sleep." Gratefully he fell asleep. He woke up the next morning, with a hell of a hangover. He knew he was going to get it then. Instead he got a cup of coffee and two headache tablets. She was dressed and she looked pretty and she smelled good. He noticed. He smelled like stale rum, cigarette smoke and sweat. He noticed that too. It felt like a flock of dirty sheep were grazing on his teeth. "I'm meeting Lucy for breakfast," she said with a minty breath, and off she went. He slept it off. He took a shower. She returned home with a beautiful bunch of flowers. He knew it would be pointless to buy her the I-am-sorry-flowers later. She had already bought them. She was in a cheerful mood. But her friendly mood was unrelated to him. This puzzled him. He initiated small talk. She responded normally. He realised she was not going to scold him about the previous night. They were not going to talk about it. He was SO relieved. She turned her back on him so he could not see the smile on her face. He told her he was going out to get pizzas. While he was away he reminded himself what a low down excuse of a husband he is and that he is lucky to have the best wife in the world. He returned with the pizza's, his favourite flavour of course, but maybe he remembered she liked pineapple. She forgave him without him having to grovel for it. Believe me, no woman, no matter what insults or foul language she uses, can make a man feel such an anti-hero and so bad about himself, than he himself can. So if he has done something bad, afford him the opportunity to reprimand himself. He will do a much better job at it and appreciate the woman much more for not doing it. Do not for one moment assume that he thinks he got away with it, or that she condoned his behaviour. He knows what he did wrong and a hero will strive to be the better man, for the woman he loves. If he perpetuates his bad behaviour, it's time to call it quits. Continuous bad behaviour means he does not want to be there anymore. Let him go.

When men hear the above case example, they all have one unanimous response. He did not do anything wrong by going out on the boys' night. He made the mistake of not informing her and not calling her when it got late. By the way, why does she want him to call her when he is out late at night or travelling? Men tend to think it is because she does not trust him – that he may be with another woman. Please! I know of men who call their wives, with their girlfriends lying right next to them. No, it is not about not trusting them. Wives want their men to call them, so she knows he is still alive. Men tend to think that they are invincible. They are warriors and their skin is made of armour. They are strong and they can look after themselves and they get irritated if women tell them to drive safely. A wife asks him to call her, not because she does not believe him to be the strong hero, she does. Rather, she asks him to call because if, heaven forbid he should die, her whole world collapses. If he dies, she is unprotected. She has no hero to protect her or to provide for her. She wants to know that he is alive, because it makes her feel safe. Feeling safe is the most basic need a woman has. So be the hero and just make the call. Just make contact.

A woman's tongue is like a dagger

Although no woman can berate a man to the same extent he can do it to himself, men also agree that the weapon a man fears most is not a dagger or a gun. It is a woman's tongue. With her tongue she can castrate him, and he has little defense. Only a woman can say: "F**k off and where the hell do you think you are going?" in the same sentence. At some point when a man and woman are yelling at each other, he tells her: "Enough." This is the point where if she was a man, he would have hit her, but he can't because she is a woman. Her words are coming at him like daggers and he is going to do something drastic to defend himself. Most men either hit the door or they leave. Then the women follow them, calling them cowards for leaving. Some men have described this as feeling as if they are being verbally violated or castrated by the woman, but they can't tell anyone about it. Or she clings to his legs and begs him not to go.

One man said: "Men do hear all the bad words. It is not necessary for her to repeat them in many different ways. When a man says "Enough, I heard you," then STOP. He will go off and consider and analyse where he went wrong. Just STOP and give him the chance to retreat."

I explain how men's bodies prepare for battle within split seconds.

26

Physiologically during a heated argument, his heart rate increases, his blood pressure rises, rushing blood to the muscle groups required for fighting and the arterioles in the skin constrict, which will reduce bleeding if he is wounded. His breathing accelerates, providing the oxygen he needs for the increased rush of blood. He starts to sweat to cool his body down in preparation for the fight. This is generally referred to as the fight-or-flight or sympathetic nervous system. These bodily adaptations require fuel. Fuel is produced by the brain alerting the adrenal glands to release adrenalin. Adrenalin produces glucose, which is the fuel required.

The neo-cortex is the part of the brain that evolved last in humans. It is responsible for choices, planning, philosophical reasoning, analytical thinking and considering long-term consequences of actions. The physiological activity of preparing the body for a fight burns the glucose, but during prolonged periods of the body under this pressure, the glucose fuel can run dry. Unfortunately, the neo-cortex, which houses self-control, also runs on glucose. Both extreme physical and mental activity can deplete the glucose reserves. This is usually when men cry ENOUGH! They know they are on the verge of losing that self-control. (Please note that this physiological explanation is by no or any means an excuse or endorsement for a man to hit a woman and any attempt to interpret it that way, will be considered malicious misinterpretation of text.)

Heated arguments

Men and women differ greatly in their expectations of each other during heated arguments. Men try to avoid verbal conflict and arguments, because words are unfamiliar weapons to them. At some point during the argument, the woman leaves, goes into the bedroom and slams the door. The man is oblivious to the fact that the woman expects him to follow her into the room. So she sits there seething and pre-navigating the next chapter of the argument in her head. The moment he walks through that door, she is just going to tell him... and he does not come through the door. Actually, he is sitting on the veranda and probably lit a fire. Fire is good for men, it has a calming effect on them. And he happened to notice the soccer score in the newspaper, which he is now reading. Men compartmentalise. Since the danger and threat of the angry woman is not currently there, he can relax. Between battles, men's bodies are relieved and cool down. (That is why we have breaks during boxing, rugby, soccer and other sporting events.) Would he for one instant consider following her into that room? You have got to be kidding! He knows what is in that room and he wants to avoid it. He actually thinks she is cooling down in that room. Meanwhile... she is seething, and the pressure is reaching boiling point. She tried crying louder, but men avoid crying women.

Eventually, unfortunately, this is also the point where some women lose the plot and threaten to harm or kill themselves in order to elicit sympathy or attention from the men. Men have a complete opposite reaction. They will assist her, take her to the hospital and get her emergency care (note: they take action, they do not express empathy) and thereafter they will try and hot heel it out of that relationship as soon as they can. Threatening or attempting suicide does not draw men closer. It repels them. I repeat: threatening or attempting suicide does not evoke feelings of empathy or love in a man. Quite the opposite.

When a woman exits a fight scene, she expects the man to come after her. When a man exits a fight, he expects the woman to let him go. Do not cling to his legs or follow him or throw objects at him.

Would it not be more productive and better for both, if women just never engage in aggressive fights with men? What is the point? There are better, more conducive and more mature ways of communicating her needs, displeasure and even her anger and hurt. There are ways to actually talk to a man, where he listens and attends to her needs. Remember, basically, men want to be the heroes and fix the women's problems.

 Read more about: TIME-OUT on page 160

"NOTHING"

Men reluctantly agree, that sometimes, they are the actual source of the woman's problem. Although usually they are the handsome, sexy, clever, strong heroes, occasionally they can be the pain in the butt or the source of her pain. They also agree that when this happens, they would

28

like her to tell them about it. I explain to the men that when she tells him about something he did that made her unhappy, men usually experience this as a dagger to the gut and then they have one of two reactions. They either say: "You are being over sensitive." Or they say: "Yes, but you also ..." In both cases they are attacking the woman and excusing or defending their own behaviour. What follows is the woman retreats into silence. The next time he sees that sullen face and he asks: "What's wrong?" he gets the icy: "Nothing." Men hate the icy note, sullen mouth, and the screwed-up eyes face. Yet, if he does not afford the woman the opportunity to communicate to him what he did to make her unhappy, without interrupting her, he is conditioning her into that sullen face.

The next time a man hears "Nothing!" from a woman, he should ask himself how he responded the previous time she tried to tell him what was upsetting her.

Tone of voice

Anyone who has watched a movie like 300, depicting the battle of Thermopylae in 480 BC when the Spartan king Leonidas faced the might of King Xerxes and the Persian empire, will develop a sense of the din of a raging battle. The man's body is geared-up in the highest fight-or-flight mode. Now in this mode, a part of the brain stem – the primitive reptile brain – secretes a neuro-modulator called noradrenalin, which peaks his aroused senses. This enables him to hear sounds in the finest detail and raises his signal-to-noise ratio. The more noise, the higher the aggression, the less he is able to argue reasonably. His pupils dilate and he is focused only on annihilating the opponent in front of him, one after the other, like a machine. Remember, his higher brain functions such as logical reasoning are temporary out of action. Would you try to reason with Leonidas in the heat of the battle? Knowing this about the functioning of a warrior, is it conducive to yell and scream at him in order to try to convince him of something?

So when I ask the men: " How would you want her to communicate to you that you did something that made her unhappy?" they all unanimously agree: "It is in the tone of voice." One of the biggest complaints men have about women is TONE OF VOICE.

Remember when I explained a man decides within split seconds preconsciously whether he is encountering an ally or an enemy? We hear faster than we see. Hearing is 25 per cent more acute than seeing. Men are especially sensitive to tone of voice, more than to content. They are also sensitive to criticism, which they perceive as verbal daggers, which will throw them into the flight-or-fight state. Men are apt not to flee, they fight.

Now the good news is if the woman is calm and engages her own parasympathetic or relaxed state, she activates her vagus nerve, which among other functions such as slowing down her breathing, will also actually lower her tone of voice. Our brains are reported to receive millions of bits of information per second from our senses, of which only 0.5 bits per second actually reaches our consciousness. The rest remain pre-conscious. So when the man perceives her calmness through his senses, he is pre-programmed to calm down and to actually stay focused and pay attention to what she is saying.

If she sits next to him, touches him and says gently: "I did not like the way you spoke to me at dinner. Please do not do it again. I do not speak to you that way." Short and sweet. No need to repeat it, or analyse it. He heard her. Maybe he will apologise there and then, probably not, but he may make her coffee later and make some silly joke just to see her smile. If he engages in some excuse or defends his actions, she should just smile and say: "I get your point. I know you don't want to hurt me deliberately. Thanks for being my hero." Now come on, can any man argue with that? Try it. It works. Much better than throwing a hissy fit and remember a gentle touch releases the oxytocin, which improves his emotional understanding of the situation.

I know women are asking: "But why should I be nice to him if he was horrible to me?" Just explain to me how reciprocating nastiness is going to resolve the problem? Or will it only exacerbate the situation? Which option offers a win-win benefit in the long run?

How would she prefer him to react when she tells him what is bothering her? She would not want him to interrupt her, defend or justify himself, change the subject or accuse her. If he could just keep quiet and let her finish talking, even if what she says may sound unfair. If she is talking in THAT TONE OF VOICE, he may say: " I really want to hear what I have done to upset you, but please can you tell me in a kinder way, it would help me understand." Then she tells him, and he listens. When she is done, he may say: "Thank you for telling me. I need time to digest this." He may even add: "I am sorry that you are hurting," if he is really kind. Then he goes off and thinks about what she said and maybe she had a point and maybe he can up his game, or maybe she had misunderstood his intentions, eventually he could consider what is more important, the issue or his marriage? The same applies to her.

I need to stress that men complain about a woman's tone of voice, but many men are guilty of raising their voices. Women are just as sensitive to men raising their voices and it scares them. Men often defend by saying they were just talking loudly. Talking loudly is raising your voice. It scares her. You are supposed to protect her, not scare her. Some men talk down to women, patronising them. Some men have a bad habit of inflicting little nasty pricks with verbal daggers, continuously sniping at their women. Prick being the operative word. This can backfire. One woman told her man: "If only your dick was as sharp as your tongue." This comment illustrates the point I made about how a man fears a woman's tongue as a dagger that can castrate him. The comment: "Since you like sex so much, don't you think it is time you learn how to do it?" has pretty much the same effect.

Perhaps men learnt to humiliate and belittle women from their mothers who used those daggers on their husbands? Imagine asking a man if he learnt to be a bitch from his mother?

Catfights

Speaking of the dagger. Women often complain that their husbands never take their side when she has an argument with his mother or another woman. I ask the woman then: "If two men were fighting each other with daggers, would you step in between them?" This is how men perceive two women fighting. If he interferes, he is going to get hurt – probably in the groin region. The secret is not to fight with another woman, but rather to lay down the weapon, move in behind her man, and trust him to protect her. He might not do it the way she wants him to (don't tell him what to do), but he will protect her. She may want him to call his mother and give her a piece of his mind. He might solve it by just keeping the two of them apart. He hates conflict, remember, and he hates being the anti-hero more. Telling his mother to butt-out makes him a major anti-hero. Please understand this. (I did not say it was fair.) Men do not like bitchy and sarcastic women. They are oblivious to the finer nuances of a catfight, but they can recognise open sarcastic, bitchy hostility and they don't like it. Most women are clever enough to stage a scene to make the other woman seem the bitch. Men never like seeing a dagger coming from a woman's mouth because they never know when it will be directed at them.

> **Case example:** One man was caught in an argument between his wife and their best female friend. He happened to agree with the other girl's point of view. "What was I supposed to do?" he asked me. "If you were at a dinner party and you made some comment that someone else disagreed with, would you want your wife to have your back, or would you want her to side with the other person against you? When we are in a partnership, we back each other up. You may just put your arm around your wife and say: "Even if I disagree with my wife's point of view, I support her right to express her opinion." Or just put your arm around her and say nothing. That would make her feel that you are protecting her, without having to agree with her."

> Remember in one of the Pirates of the Caribbean movies, where the mermaids hang on to the rowing boats of the pirates, and they have the sweetest, serene, beautiful faces and suddenly they open their mouths revealing their terrible fangs? That pretty much describes what happens when that TONE OF VOICE and the daggers emerge.

Check out men's profiles on dating sites. What is the one major off-putting characteristic they all agree on? Sarcasm.

> Case example: A man walks up to his girlfriend at a social function. He asks if he can get her a refill. "I thought you'd never ask. You would let me die of thirst here," she says and holds her glass out to him. He will refill her drink and hand it to her silently. And he will pick a fight with her on the way home and he will probably just drop her off at the

gate. What if she had just smiled and said: "Thanks, you're my hero." He would have been attentive and affectionate towards her and all the other women would have complained to their husbands and boyfriends asking why could they not be more like that man who clearly adores his girlfriend?

Ask nicely

Case example: The woman says: "You know," wagging her finger in the air, "you would walk past this smelly dustbin and not even think of taking it out. I have to do everything in this house." Then she wonders why he just looks at her and then resumes watching television. What happened to: "Would you please take out the dustbin for me, it is heavy and smelly." His first reaction would probably be: "Must I do it now?" (I told you it is not fair.) Then she responds: "Yes please, I want to start dinner and it is smelly and I am sure you are hungry too." If she smiles when she asks, he will do it. When he returns and she thanks him for being her hero, he will probably hang around the kitchen and ask if there is anything else he can do to help her. Ask him to peel the onions. Why don't women just ask nicely when they want men to do something for them?

Why do women think they have to manipulate to get something? Ask nicely, charm a little and stroke his ego, it works better. Men are not stupid. They know when they are being manipulated and they resent it. They also know when they are being charmed and they love it. Just be sincere. If she does not want to stroke his ego and be charming towards him, what is she doing there? Is this not the man she is supposed to be in love with? The more truly feminine she is, the more she activates the hero. If he does not respond with heroic actions, leave.

One woman asked: "So must I continuously lick his boots to get him to do something?" "No, just ask nicely," I answered. "Must I then continuously praise him and tell him he is my hero?" she asked. "Why not? You did it when you dated. You married your hero. Why not remind him of it? What do you have to lose? You may just regain your hero."

One man explains: "Please don't lose the praising. You will profit double in return and other women will envy the way he spoils you."

The male apology

Many women expect men to verbally apologise or agree with them. Why? He is a man, he has an ego – which is a good thing – why insist on a verbal apology? It is not his language. He is action orientated. He will SHOW her he is sorry by filling her car with petrol, buying her flowers, or just doing something for her. Once she understands this, and acknowledges the act of apology, without insisting on the verbal apology, he will thank his lucky stars for being with the best woman in the world and he will endeavour to spoil her more.

> **Case example:** A couple had a huge argument at a friend's house. As they approached the garden gate on their way out, the man stopped and picked a flower. "We must get you a plant like this," he said and offered her the flower. She slapped the flower from his hand. What she did not realise was that the offering of the flower was his way of apologising. Men would much rather express themselves through such an action, than with a verbal apology. It is the way they are.

Many men told me they do not always expect a woman to say she is sorry if she did something that offended him. They rather want her to understand why he was offended. For example, discussing his shortcomings with his friends is excruciatingly embarrassing to a warrior. Betraying his secrets and embarrassing him in company are some of the worst offences.

Fighting his battles

Remember men are warriors. Some women, however, think they can snatch the sword from his hand and fight the battle for him. (He wants her to be able to fight her own battles when he is not there, but do not fight his battles when he is present.) When this occurs, he will either attack her, or sit back and watch her make a fool of herself. Men usually have a reaction: "Well then, see if you can do it better, but do not come running to me if you get hurt." Battlefield is male territory, if a woman engages in battle, she becomes a comrade or an enemy, not the woman he needs to protect. And he wants to be with a woman whom he can protect, because it makes him feel good. What makes the woman think she can handle his situation better?

> **Case example:** A man and his girlfriend approached the client liaison officer at the bank. The man explained that he wanted to switch bank accounts. The client liaison officer was a bit haughty. The girlfriend stepped up from behind him, pushed her way in front, wagged her finger at the liaison officer and told her her fortune. The man left the bank. The girlfriend said she just tried to help. Soon after, he left the girlfriend too. Men do not require women to take up arms for them. They need women to back them up. The emphasis is on Stay back.

Another milder example of snatching the sword from his hand would be a couple sitting at a table in a restaurant and the waiter taking his time to attend to them. Then the woman waives a waiter over or worse, gets up and fetches a waiter to the table. Sit back, lady, relax. He has it under control. She will get her food and he will pay for it too. It may be a good idea as well to tell the man what she would like to order instead of directly to the waiter. Men look forward to treating a lady to dinner. It presents them with an opportunity to be a hero, to treat her and spoil her. It is not that he is buying your gratitude, because he is paying for dinner, it is more just a matter of good manners to show genuine appreciation. Is it really too much to ask to make him feel like the hero? I think not.

Heroes never kick the bunny

When I was still a profiler, a commander of a murder-and-robbery unit invited me to his house. He wanted to show me something. The detectives were quite curious, so we all went along. He showed me his children's bunny. I held the bunny and stroked its ears. The men were mesmerized. I put the bunny down and it hopped around on the lawn. Their gazes followed the bunny. When the bunny approached one of them, the others would caution him to watch out for the bunny. I realised there is a code of honour among men: No one kicks the bunny. They protect the bunny and they feel good protecting the bunny. I am not advocating that women should hop around the lawn, but since women have a deep-seated need to feel safe, what is wrong with activating the protector and making the men feel good about it? It is a win-win.

The last word on men and action: A man has got to do what a man has got to do. Do not stand in his way, rather trust that he will do it well, and he may just want to come home to you, without you having to try and catch him.

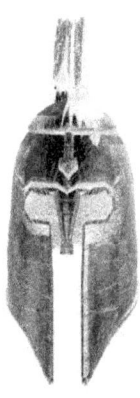

GENEROUS HEROES: PROVIDERS

The psychologist Maslow formulated the well-known theory of the hierarchy of needs, shaped like a pyramid. At first base are our basic physiological needs, such as hunger, sex, warmth and sleep. The second tier of the pyramid represents the need for safety. The third is the need to belong – to be loved. Fourth is the need for self-esteem, to feel good about ourselves and fifth is the need for self-actualisation – the altruistic need to surpass our individual needs, to become the best person we can be. When I investigated serial killers, I found that most male serial killers killed for sex, the first base. The female serial killers, on the other hand, killed for money.

This is interesting and I explored the concept. A little girl recognises her father as the PROVIDER. He goes out to work, earns a salary and provides the roof over her head and brings home the bacon. So in a sense, she equates his love with money and this is also how men generally express their love to their families. By providing. Having the home and the food and the stuff her father's money can buy, makes her feel safe and being cared for. If in some sense her father disappointed her, or rejected her, she will always subconsciously hunt the money, as a substitute to fill the empty void which the lack of his love created in her. In some extreme cases where the father molested his daughter or abandoned her, the yearning for money as a substitute for his love and protection, may become so all-consuming that she will kill for it. To women, money represents safety.

 Read more about: MASLOW'S HIERARCHY OF NEEDS on page 162

To men, money represents status

Men feel good about themselves when they are good providers. It boosts their self-esteem. That is how I came to realise that to men money represents status – the fourth tier of Maslow's hierarchy. Money for women represents a basic need – safety. The second tier of the pyramid. Men need sex and women need to feel safe. Men agree they would rather lose their women to another man with more money, than to a man who is better in bed.

In antiquity a man's worth was measured by his bravery and valour. His physical strength and performance as a warrior earned him the respect and perhaps the envy of other men. Power was embedded in strength. In our age, men judge other men by their wealth. Money has become the benchmark of a man's worth. It is the mighty magnates who rule the world, not the politicians, nor the kings.

Rings and shiny things

Why do men buy their wives and girlfriends jewelry? So she can wear it at home? No, so she can wear it for other people to see what a good provider he is. Men like women to show off their wealth. Of course, most women do not complain, but often when I see rich men's wives and their fingers sparkle with several huge diamond rings, I tend to wonder; the more rings, the less attention she gets. "I-will-make-it-up-to-you rings." Most of those women will exchange those rings at any given moment for more quality time and personal attention from their husbands.

Men are aware of the fact that society expects them to provide. That is often why so many of them avoid marriage – they are not ready to take on the responsibility of providing. However, some men make the mistake of thinking all women are gold diggers. (Some women are and some are spoilt brats, but I will get to that later.) Many women are quite content when the basics are covered. If they have a roof, food, clothes and most of all safety, especially when they reach old age, they are happy. A little spoiling is appreciated but honestly, not all of them demand or require the diamond rings. Men tend to think women require the luxuries, because it suits the men to think so, because it makes them feel good when they can afford it.

> **Case example:** One man promised himself he would not ask a girl to marry him, unless he could provide for her better than her father. He dated his high school sweetheart and when he could finally afford to buy her a house, he married her. By then he was already in his thirties. Later he became a very wealthy man. When his daughter turned 21, he wanted to buy her a house. I reminded him of his promise to himself. "If you buy your daughter an expensive house, you are raising the bar too high for her potential husband and she will end up a lonely rich Daddy's little girl. You spoil your daughter's chances." He bought her a small flat.

Men want women to spend their money, when they offer it. They only require the woman to be appreciative and not to waste it.

> **Case example:** A rich man became irate when his wife "squirreled" the spending money he gave her. He gave her an excessive monthly allowance and when they went abroad, he often handed her wads of cash to "buy a handbag or something pretty." She banked the money. Also, her main complaint was that there was never enough money, despite the fact that they lived in a multi-million mansion and she drove a German sports car. I

explained to him the principle that she felt unsafe. If a woman feels unsafe, no amount of money will compensate for it. She did not know if that house or car was paid-up, whether the bailiff could repossess it, or if he had made provision for her and their children, should something happen to him. So she lived frugally and saved the money. Once he explained his finances to her and showed her that she would be taken care of in retirement, she relaxed. He even transferred one of the properties into her name.

I have often witnessed the gilded cage syndrome. A wealthy man will thwart every attempt of his wife to earn her own money. "She does not need to work, I provide for her," he proclaims, but deep down he cannot tolerate the idea of her gaining independence, for he fears she may leave him. Is he not, by keeping her in the gilded cage and withholding her independence, acknowledging his own insecurity that she may not love him for the man he is? Does he never consider that she may stay, because she loves him as a man, and not because he keeps her captive in golden chains? Often when these women do something to displease the man, he threatens to throw her out, cut off her finances and even abandon her family members he may have been providing for as well. Would he not rather be the man she would voluntarily want to be with, even if he was not wealthy at all? Sometimes I encourage these men to support their wives in establishing their own financial independence, for that would provide the final proof of whether she stays with him for the money, or for himself.

Some women, however, spend his money as if there is no tomorrow. I sometimes wonder at the ease with which these women consider their husbands' wallets as the proverbial widow's flask that just never runs dry. They help themselves with no thought or consideration of the fact that that money is earned by hard work. He WORKS for it. He gets up at 5am, while she is still snoozing, and he returns home after 8pm, when she is again in her pyjamas, (or still in her pyjamas). I know I am exaggerating, but I have seen many such examples. Worse, there are women who presume they are entitled to an unlimited access to the money, because they "run" the house or raise his children. "Excuse me, but are they not your children too? Do you require to be paid or compensated to rear your own children? Are you the Nanny earning a

40

salary?" Consider the single Moms out there who work hard to raise their own children and who do not have the luxury of a double income family. They do not expect to be paid to raise their children. I do not contest when families have the arrangement that the men work and earn the money and that the women stay at home and raise the children and that this in itself is very hard work. I do not contest that is a good 50 – 50 partnership agreement. But some women have a hell-of-a-self-righteous attitude to this set-up. Some women become extremely indignant when the husband requires some form of bookkeeping as to what his money was spent on and if he requests that she should stick to a budget. Here is a tip, ladies: It is not unreasonable for a man to require quotes or cash slips as proof of expenditure. He is not obliged to hand over wads of cash or pay limitless accounts. He is not being spiteful, it is just called responsible financial management. He has a right to know what you are doing with his money, just as you have a right to ask him about financial affairs concerning you.

> **Case example:** A woman complained that her husband buys lavish gifts for their young adult children. She was concerned that they, as a couple, may suffer during their retirement. The wife did not work. She was a stay-at-home-Mom, but the children had all moved out of the home. I asked her if she needed anything. She reflected for a moment and admitted she had a good home, a car, clothes, food etc. They lived a moderate middle-class life, but she needed nothing. Since the children were grown up and had left the home, she could sleep late and she spent most of her days updating her Facebook Page, playing computer games, cleaning the house and preparing dinner. Eventually she concluded: "I sound like a spoilt brat." I agreed. "He gets up at 5 in the morning, brings you coffee in bed and he goes off to work. He provides for you. He works hard for his money so why on earth can he not spend it on something that makes him happy – even if that entails gifts for his children?" I agreed that the children are spoilt, but it remains his prerogative to spend some of his money on whatever he wants, does it not? If she requires some luxuries, why does she not get up at 6 am and go to

work as well? With her earnings she can contribute to the existing life insurance policies if she was so concerned about their retirement. Instead of criticising the man for not earning enough, she could support him by finding employment. She complained she had been out of the market for too long and she was too old to work. I assured her even if she found a job for R3 000 a month, it would cover her petrol and could add up to a considerable premium and savings. Her alternative is to stay at home, sleep late, clean her home, cook dinner, play computer games and thank her husband for being the provider hero he is, and to stop complaining.

The flip side of the coin: Sometimes men also have the inclination to think that because they pay for everything, they own the woman.

Case example: An affluent man bought his wife a little sports car. One day he took the car in for a service. The salesman offered him a trade-in on the car and an amount of cash. As the man could do with the cash at that moment, he traded the car. He could not understand why his wife was upset. I explained to him that he had negated her right to ownership, by selling her car, without even discussing it with her. He treated her like a slave, who had no right to possession. He answered that since he had paid for the car in the first place, and since he was in charge of the finances, he could sell the car. She should trust him that he needed the cash then and that he could buy her another newer model sports car later. I explained that he sold her possession. He answered: "So my money is our money – she has free access to it, but what is hers is only hers?" The mistake lay in the lack of communication. If only he had asked or even just told her what he planned to do, she probably would have agreed to it. Men regard communication as the most important part of a relationship, yet often they fail to communicate.

The psychologist Carl Jung formulated the concept of a collective subconscious. Since women have been suppressed for millennia, they developed a collective subconscious memory of it and resistance to it. Women are sensitive when their rights as humans are not respected. They have a right to an opinion, to property, to work, to love, etc. One man said he understands this deep-seated issue and he could understand why she gets upset when he uses her stuff (like her car) without asking her permission. He can respect her right to "Mine", even when he paid for it, but he wished she would not rub his nose in her "ownership" so often. He wished she could tone it down a little. Noted.

Smile

What appreciation do men need for providing? Work is the battlefield where he fights the dragons and at the end of the day wins the prizes to bring home to his wife. So he gets home after a long day, and she hardly greets him, she is busy doing something else, or she cannot wait to tell him about her problems. Could she please... just ... smile. Not fake it, mean it. Can she smile at the man whom she loves? (I can already hear the women complaining: "I work hard too, when I get home in the afternoons, I am also tired..." There you go, complaining again, with a sullen face. Just the kind of woman a man cannot wait to come home to?)

Men are born with the innate need to provide and protect. When a mother holds her baby boy in her arms, she smiles at him and he knows the world is perfect. The moment she frowns, although he is still pre-verbal, he tries to figure out what he can do to make her happy. Men want to know they make women happy. They will act like clowns and do all kinds of silly things, just to entertain her and see her smile. Once she smiles at him, he gets the message: "You are doing your job well. I am happy." Then he can relax. In so many relationships that run into trouble, the women have stopped smiling at the men. When he comes home at night, just give him a smile first. It makes it all worthwhile.

Many men eventually feel they are just the wallet in the home. They are no longer appreciated, they feel no matter how hard they try, they just never get it right, as she always moves the goal posts. The sad thing is, many of these men stay in the marriages because they do not want to leave her in the lurch. They just try harder and grow more and more unhappy. They no longer like or love her, but they cannot leave her because no one kicks the bunny, remember. Especially if she no longer listens to him and he has gone all quiet and she only uses him as a wallet, and most probably no longer sleeps with him. This is the point where many men cry: "Enough". And they walk out. Sometimes to another woman who is appreciative and needs him to be the hero, sometimes just because he has had enough. I often ask women if they thank their husbands at the end of the month for providing for them, for paying the bond, etc. The women answer: "Why should I? It is his job." Yet, these same women get upset when the husband does not thank her for cooking him a meal every night.

One man said: "I know when my relationships are heading for the pits. She stops kissing me passionately and she gets that expression of discontent. I just break up before she gets to the never-ending-complaining phase."

> **Case example**: The wife wanted her husband not to work so late and to come home earlier. When he walked in after 8pm, she shouted at him and smashed the plates of food on the floor. Without replying, he turned around and set off to the local pub, where he had dinner and a couple of beers. When he got home eventually, he was too drunk to care whether she picked a fight or not. This woman was doing a 180-degrees opposite of what she wanted. She wanted him to come home. Why would he want to come home to a banshee? When she stopped her antics and welcomed him home one night with a candlelit dinner and a smile, he came home early after that. He said he did not expect a candlelit dinner every night, he just wanted her to stop fighting and be nice and smile. He worked late because he provided for them. Some men work very late because they want to avoid the banshee at home.

Remember when I explained that when a woman smiles at a man, within split seconds on a pre-conscious level, he relaxes and treats her like an ally? Here is another benefit of smiling: Our faces reveal micro expressions at such a rate, we are hardly conscious of them and we respond to other people's micro expressions mostly on a pre-conscious level. It is rather uncanny that the vagus nerve, which regulates the parasympathetic (relaxed) nervous system originates from the same part of the brain stem which regulates our facial muscles. The moment we

44

relax our facial muscles into a smile, we send a message to our gut to relax and our heart rate to slow down. So even if we feel depressed or down, a smile and deep breathing will send a message to the brain to generate positive thoughts. You can smile yourself happy. Men are drawn to happy women, because it makes their job at making her happy so much easier.

Neuroscientists discovered mirror neurons in the brain. A simple example would be that we all tend to yawn when we see someone else yawning. These neurons cause us to understand the meaning of another person's behaviour and bring us in touch with that feeling. When we watch a moving scene in a movie, we tend to cry along. Interestingly women have more mirror neurons than men, meaning women are much more emotionally empathic in touch, and able to read emotional facial expressions. However due to their status as warriors and protectors, men are far better equipped to read and interpret negative facial emotions. A frown or a scowl on a woman's face triggers an automatic attack mode in a man, while a smile or gentle expression, will trigger the protection mode.

To show appreciation to a Provider, just smile.

Gifts

Parents have reported to me when they give pocket money to girls, they spend it fast. However, boys save their pocket money – so they can spend it on girls later. Sweet.

It is not a good idea for a woman to buy a man expensive presents, especially not before he has bought her a gift first. I asked the men what would be typical signs that a boy likes a girl. They all answered: "He buys her things." Men like to make grand gestures and impress the women with expensive gifts like a car, or a diamond ring. Usually it is something other people will notice. For in the eyes of other men, he is a good provider. Men like to receive presents, but what they like better are daily gestures that she is thinking of him and that he is special to her. For heaven's sake, this only applies when they are in a relationship. Showering him with little gifts every day while he is still making up his mind about her, is not a good idea. He does not want to feel bought. He wants to make up his own mind. He wants to do the buying. Little tokens of appreciation once there is an established relationship, is good. Like buying him 2 per cent milk because he likes it, or his favourite flavoured biltong (jerky), or replacing his cologne when it is almost finished, because she noticed. As soon as she gives him a big expensive gift, she is competing with him on his level. He wants her to be in awe of him, not to compete with him. Men like to impress women, not to compete with them. Again, it may not be fair, but it is the way it is. Many men claim they do not mind if the woman earns a bigger salary, but believe me, deep down, most of them do. Even if they accept it, they resent it when she makes it obvious.

Some men think it is fine to ask their personal assistants to buy a gift for their wives. It is not. The only time when it is acceptable to ask a third party to get involved, is when you order her flowers from a florist, long distance since you could not deliver it yourself. It is acceptable to ask your sister or the wife's best friend to go along and help you chose a gift, but often they may get it wrong. She would rather have something not quite 100 per cent her taste, but completely chosen by you, than have someone else choose it for her. It is the thought and your effort that count. Men would like to see the woman not only appreciate the gift, but also to use it, wear it and show it off. Do not spare the expensive perfume. He intended it for his woman's pleasure. To make her happy. If she spares it, she is conveying the message that she does not believe he will earn enough to replace it. If she really, really dislikes it, she can tell him – nicely – and exchange it. She can take him along and make him feel special for spoiling her. It is not a good idea to tell the shop assistant: "My husband always gets it wrong."

In a league of her own

Men observe women and at a glance decide whether they can afford her or not. They call it a league. This league is linked to his earning capacity. Some men prefer women in a higher league for it inspires them to raise the bar, to step up and to fulfil their potential. Some men prefer women in a lower league, so she will be grateful for what he can afford. It makes it easier for him. Some women fall in love with men who cannot afford them, because those men may have other qualities that are far more important to the woman, than his bank balance. However, these men may develop inferiority complexes, because men generally benchmark

46

their success on their earning capacity. Heroes despise unemployed men who live off women. It is called pimping.

Some men like dating financially successful women, because it affirms that he can afford that league. Few men, but they do exist, are not intimidated by a woman's earning capacity or her bank balance. It actually inspires him, rather than threatens him. These men have the self-confidence to believe in themselves and they do not need to rely on their bank balances to impress. There is a difference between self-confidence and arrogance. Earning her own salary contributes to a woman's independent status.

Men prefer women to be the medium for showing off their success. Many men think they do not deserve to spoil themselves. It does them good to hear that they do.

> **Case example:** An affluent man had a problem acknowledging his success. No matter how much he earned, he felt it was never enough. This was not due to his wife. She adored him and was very appreciative. He grew up in a home where he could never please his mother. I suggested he buy himself a present so he can be reminded of his material success on a daily basis. It took some time to convince him that he deserved to spoil himself. Eventually he confessed that he liked fancy cars. I asked him if he would like to spoil himself with a new sports car. "If I drive that thing on the highway, all the other chaps will think I am an arrogant bragging dick," he said. "Or they may think, wow, check that guy, he made it. If I work harder, I might make it too," I answered, " your success may just inspire them. You have earned the car. You reached the bar." One morning he arrived in a Jaquar sports car. "My wife said it looked sexy," he said shyly. I agreed.

Footing the bill

> **Case example:** One man complained every time he took his friends out to dinner, his wife would grab the bill and

check if the waiter had over-charged him, or she would calculate the other couples' share. She is overtly sending his guests the message that he cannot afford it and that he is a bad provider. This is a major insult to a hero.

Many women wonder if they should offer to pay half of the restaurant bill. Men agree that she can offer once, because it creates the impression that she does not believe she is entitled to his money, but when he says No, she should not embarrass him by insisting. She is creating the impression that he cannot afford her. He would not have invited her if he could not afford her. It is fine if she invites him now and again, but men do feel uncomfortable when women settle a bill in public. Best to pay the bill when he goes to the bathroom. They suggest she can rather treat him to a home cooked meal, or she can take him on a picnic. Then she provides the food and the ambiance, and he is not put on the spot in public. When they are just friends, they can share the bill or take turns in paying, but it still makes the man feel uncomfortable.

Just as a woman is not entitled to his money, so he is not entitled to her body when he pays for dinner.

A woman's validation of her man's success is very important, whatever his league.

Remember to a man money represents status, to a woman it represents security. Some men earn smaller salaries, but they work hard, and they have generous hearts. Blessed are their girlfriends and wives who appreciate them for the heroes they are. Men can also understand some women love them for who you are, not for what you earn.

HEROES ON THEIR QUESTS

Ancient Greek mythology relates many tales of heroes pursuing their quests. The hero Thesseus slew the Minotaur in the labyrinth on Crete. His lover, the King's daughter and chief priestess, Ariadne, gave him a ball of thread which guided him out of the labyrinth. He promised to marry her. However, Thesseus left her on the island Naxos and sailed away to follow his destiny to become the King of Athens. Heartbroken Ariadne turned to Dionysos, the god of drink and lust, and she joined a band of women who reveled in wild orgies, drank too much and devoured men. (Thesseus later married her little sister Phaedra, who fell in love with her stepson!)

Medea also used her powers as a priestess to provide magic and herbs to the hero Jason on his quest to find the golden fleece. He married her and they had two sons. Then he followed his quest and abandoned her in favour of the daughter of King Creon of Corinth, princess Glauke. Medea killed their sons and killed princess Glauke with a poisoned dress. She also killed her brother who tried to stop her and eventually she married Thesseus' father and attempted to kill Thesseus.

Odysseus, King of Ithica, a little island to the west of Greece, was one of the Achaean heroes of the Trojan war. He survived the 10-year war on the shores of Illium, but when he sailed home, he got lost for another 10 years. So for 20 years his wife, Queen Penelope, faithfully ruled his kingdom in his absence and waited for him, despite many suitors vying to win her hand. Noble Odysseus, we think, deserves such a faithful wife, until we read Homer's Odyssey and learn that seven of those 10 lost years Odysseus spent in the arms of the seductress and siren Calypso. He later contested that he wanted to leave, as he yearned for Penelope. Poor Odysseus?

One of the few Trojans who survived the war was the Trojan hero Aneas. He escaped with his life and fled to Carthage, where he fell in love with the beautiful Queen Dido. They consummated their love in a cave and she understood this to be a proposal of marriage. Aneas abandoned her and set off on his quest to found Rome. She killed herself.

Get the picture? Women assume sex is a declaration of everlasting love or a marriage proposal. Also, when a woman stands in the way of a man's quest, she gets left behind, despite the fact that he may love her. Abandoned and rejected women go on the rebound, commit suicide or get very, very nasty. Women want love, men want glory. Women believe love conquers all. Men do not. Men believe they can conquer the world.

Love of your life?

Heroes have a quest. It drives them. Despite everything. They need to find and follow this passion, this quest. Sometimes the quest is off the beaten track, like becoming a famous photographer, or a hunter – remember Robert Redford's character in the movie Out of Africa – but mostly it involves their career and making money. It is the number one priority. The woman or the wife is not the number one priority. She may become a main distraction for a while, but she is not the lifelong priority. She may become the end to the means – some men realise eventually to amass such riches and to have no one to share it with (or to spend it on) is meaningless and his wife or family becomes the end to the means. The quest / passion / job remains the means to the end though. Speaking metaphorically, a man may feel that he needs a four-carat diamond before he can rightfully and honourably stand in front of a woman and ask her to marry him. "What if she is the love of your life and you may lose her if you go off on this quest? What if she says she does not need a four-carat diamond, she just wants you?" I ask. All the men I asked responded exactly the same... they just shrugged their shoulders. "You stand to lose the love of your life. You will never get another love like this, ever?" "So be it," they all answer without exception. Pose this question to a woman and she will sacrifice anything and drop everything, including her panties, for the love of her life.

The right woman at the right time at the right place. The right woman, the wrong time and wrong place; no go. She may be the woman he wants to marry, but if he is not ready to get married, he WILL LET HER GO. She remembers the wonderful times they shared when they were in love, the promises he made and how all of that just evaporated one day in a flash. She asks herself: "Does he not love me? " He does. But it is not enough. She may make the perfect wife, but if he does not want to get married, that will not convince him. She may be Miss Right, but if he is Mr Not Ready, he will leave her and avoid her, even if it breaks his heart and it certainly breaks her heart.

Love is not enough, if a man is not ready. She may sleep with him, to rekindle his feelings, and of course he will sleep with her, because he loves her and she is offering herself to him, but that will not make him stay. HE WILL STILL LEAVE. He will avoid her so as not to witness her heartbreak, he will emerge himself in work to be too busy or too tired to think of her, and the last thing she should do is run after him or tell him he is the love of her life. He knows. He does not want to hear it. He is not ready. Hitch your horses, lady, and move on. He does not want to get hitched. IF HE IS NOT READY, IT IS NOT GOING TO HAPPEN.

> **Case example:** One man was an ardent sportsman and trained for the Olympics. He met a young woman who stunned him from the first moment he saw her. She lived in another town. He did not pursue the relationship, for he was focused on his training and could not afford the effort

51

of maintaining a long-distance relationship and train for the Olympics. She carried on living her own life. Six months later, they met up again. He realised she was the love of his life. Guess what? They dated for a year and he broke up with her because the relationship was getting too serious and he was pursuing a gold medal. Again, she did not wait for him. She carried on with her life. Did he miss her? Yes, he did! Did he kick his own butt for losing her? Yes, he did! Did he saddle his horse and go looking for the love of his life? No. A year later he ran into her for the third time. By this time, he had earned his gold medal. He felt worthy of standing in front of her and asked her to be his wife. They are still happily married today. He can count himself lucky and favoured by the gods.

Free spirits

Men need to hunt, to seek, to embark on a quest, and eventually to leave a legacy. Some of them develop the common sense to realise there need to be people or just a person to appreciate that legacy, whatever it is, else it would be lost and turn into dust and that would be a sorry state of affairs. It may also be more meaningful when there is a woman who accompanies him to witness his journey, inspire him, record it, appreciate it, see it, praise him and to believe in him. Sometimes these women may be free spirits themselves, who can align their own destinies or purpose with his without smothering him, dampening his spirits or tying him down. Some woman can be the wind beneath his wings, and not the ball and chain around his ankles. These are the independent women all men say they yearn for, but whom few men can actually truthfully handle. These are the women who embrace their femininity, who do not want to be the better man, who do not regard praising him as the hero as a denigrating experience. These are women who are in touch with their inner goddess and celebrate the liberation of a man being the man. They are not helpless, needy, dependent, greedy, devious, cynical, or manipulating, but they do need heroes. Real heroes, who man-up to the challenge of being her man. These women are not interested in relationships with immature men. They are not out to catch men. In their view a relationship need not necessarily lead to a lifelong commitment, but it does need to be a solid relationship and it may even last a life time.

I digressed but now I return to the point that men will give up the love of their lives to follow their quests, that love is not their main priority. "They got married and they lived happily ever after", is the ending of women's fantasy fairy tales. "Riding off into the sunset on his trusty steed"' or "going down in a blaze of glory,'" like Butch and Sundance is the ending of cowboy novels. (If you do not know who Butch and Sundance were, you may be too young to read this book.)

I pause here to allow this phenomenon to sink in....

The men answer they may lose the love of their lives when they are not ready for her. She may marry another man. He may meet and marry another woman and secretly always pine for his lost love, thinking she is better off without him. Very noble. I am sure Queen Penelope felt the same.

The point is a man wants a woman who can align with his quest. Aligning with the quest does not mean hijacking the quest or abandoning hers to sheepishly follow his. He needs a woman who understands the importance of the quest. It makes him the better man and she needs to inspire him to that pinnacle of manhood. She needs to understand this need of his and not stand in his way or fight it or criticise him or blame him for striving towards it. He certainly resents her nagging him to do something else, like marrying her.

Usually this quest is represented by his work, but it may be an ambition or a passion or a secret dream like sailing the seven seas.

Case example: A CEO of his own company takes his wife to dinner in a fancy restaurant. His cell phone rings. "I have to take this, there is a crisis at the workshop." He spends a good 20 minutes on the phone on the balcony of the restaurant. She sits alone at the table, waiting. When he returns, she has either left the restaurant or she is furious and starts bickering, or she has the icy sullen face. He is definitely not getting sex that night. Men want women to understand that that 20-minute phone call is what pays for that fancy dinner. Women want men to understand she would rather have a hamburger at Wimpy and his undivided attention for one night. The woman who does not complain, but orders his favourite meal, or asks the kitchen to keep it warm for him, is the one who understands the quest. She gets him. He will make it up to her. Maybe with a holiday in Santorini. Sounds fair to me.

His turf

It is not a good idea for a wife to work at her husband's company. Work is the battlefield where men earn their stripes. It is the stage where he earns the money to provide. It is an integral important aspect of his life. If he owns the company, then it is also his domain. It is the last place where he needs a woman to boss him around and to tell him what to do. He is the boss. He may discipline her as he does any other employee, and boy is he going to pay later tonight for humiliating her in front of everybody. Unfortunately very, very few and virtually none of the wives can actually get it right to be just another employee at her husband's company. The same applies to children working for their parents, but sometimes to a lesser extent. The wife may not boss her husband around at work, but other personnel know she is the boss' wife. If she is five minutes late and he ignores it, they cry foul. Sometimes she is sweet and nice and hugs him. Men cringe at this. It makes him seem weak and vulnerable, not the boss. Sometimes she thinks and behaves as if she is the boss. She even talks about "our company". She may be the beneficiary of the profit of that company, but if he is the boss, then it is not her company.

Taking or even just talking co-ownership of his company makes him seem incompetent. It is deadly. Do not do it. It is his quest. He leads. Support his quest, share it if you may, but do not hi-jack it.

> **Case example**: One woman complained that her husband volunteered to work extra shifts on weekends. She did not like it because she wanted to spend time with him, but she understood he did this to increase his income. She accepted it. One Sunday afternoon when he had the day off and they enjoyed a snooze, they were interrupted by a call from a female colleague at work, who needed assistance. He had to be the hero at work and if he said no, he would be the anti-hero. She wanted her husband to be her hero and stay with her. She did not want him to be the female colleague's hero. Now we have a conflict of interests here. This can easily develop into a power game. If she had insisted that he stayed at home, she would have been doing that thing where women tell men what to do. This would have alienated him. He would probably have gone to work, just to prove to her that he is a man who can go where he wants to. And he may have stopped at a pub on the way home, because he wanted to avoid the sulking wife at home. Alternatively, she decided to accompany him to work and made him a happy man while he was driving there. Just to remind him where his priorities lay and to show support for his quest. I did not say it is fair, but he was reminded that he had married the best girl in the world. And the female colleague got the message that this was a happily married man.

Often working women give up their jobs to become stay-at-home-Moms. Some of them have the luxury of au pairs and housekeepers who mainly drive the kids around and tend to the house. The women become bored and lonely. They envy the men their exciting lives, surrounded by other intelligent, dynamic people, who dress up in suits in the morning. The women cut their hair in short functionable hairdos and wear ridiculous Capri pants that reach halfway down their calves and flat sandals that show off their pedicures. But they long for the hustle and bustle of working life, of making deals and they resent the high-powered women colleagues or pretty sales reps with their long hair, who cross the paths of their men. The wives do lunch with their equally bored friends, they have their nails done, their eyelines tinted, their eyebrows plucked, and they have set appointments at the hairdresser every week. They frequent coffee shops, chatting to the baristas, ordering designer cupcakes, reading novels or fashion magazines or updating their Facebook, just to escape their homes. (Very few of them actually read the newspapers in these coffee shops.) Eventually they become bored out of their skulls and then they begin to deliberately pick fights with their husbands at night. Just to get his attention and because they envy his power-charged, interesting life. They sabotage the men on their quests by sending them hundreds of emails or sms'or whats-apps during the day, demanding his immediate attention to an irrelevant problem. If he does not respond, she throws a tantrum, accuses him of not loving her, or having an affair with a colleague or causes some drama for him to resolve. JUST TO GET HIS ATTENTION.

These women are not aligned with their men's quests. When I suggest they get a job, they all answer they do not need to work, because the husband supports them, or the husband would not approve of it. These are the women who grow emotionally and financially dependent on the man, and then punishes him for it. Having to keep her entertained after a long day on the battlefield drains him. One woman answered: "If he buys me a coffee shop or something, I would not be able to travel so much." She travelled abroad at least three or four times a year, at his expense, without him. She attended cooking classes in Tuscany. If he was not home by 8pm at night, she chucked the food in the dustbin, because he did not appreciate the effort she made to cook it! If these women refuse to work, why don't they get involved in charity? the men ask. Why can't women find something meaningful to do with their lives? the men want to know.

Men appreciate women who have a passion or an interest of their own. It makes the man very nervous when that passion or interest is him. A man does not want a woman's whole life to revolve around him. It ties him down. It overloads him with expectancies. It is too much. However, once he marries her, he does want her to take care of the household requirements, pick up the mail and do the groceries, collect his prescription medication and dry-cleaning, tend to the childrens' extracurricular activities, send flowers and a birthday card to his mother, take the dog to the vet, need him like a hero and please just maintain her own interest as well. He also wants her undivided attention when he is present. I did not say it is fair.

A last word on quest: When the three goddesses Hera, Athena and Aphrodite presented the Trojan prince, Paris, with a choice of the throne of Asia and Europe; wisdom and the acclaim of being a great warrior; or the most beautiful woman in the world Helen, to become the love of his life, he chose Helen. The mighty city of Troy was doomed for his choice of love over power and glory, and he was branded a coward among men. When Achilles was given the choice of a long and happy family life or a short life crowned by eternal glory as the greatest warrior, he chose the latter. That is why men regarded him as a Hero.

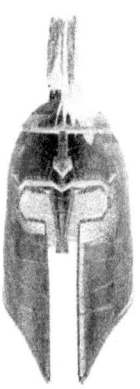

HEROES IN LOVE

People in love are playful, like puppies, and a puppy is the cutest thing. Most women adore the smell of a puppy's breath. If only someone could produce cologne smelling like puppy breath, women would follow men everywhere. Puppies grow into loyal dogs and our best friends. They play with us and protect us. However, a puppy will wee on your carpet, it will dig out the plants in your garden and if you leave the gate open long enough, it will run after the bitch down the road. We decide that despite this we still want the puppy. Relationships are similar. There are certain characteristics about men that make them men and it may not be fair, and women cannot change it. And vice versa. For instance: Men do not do emotions. Women do emotions. If men do not like women's emotions, then men should date other men.

Ever heard of the expression: people fall in love, because there is chemistry between them? Not to spoil the fun, but there are specific parts of our brains at play when we fall in love. When we notice an attractive person for the first time, the left pre-frontal cortex alerts us to pay attention to this person and we experience positive thoughts about him or her. The right pre-frontal cortex – responsible for negative thoughts – is temporarily disabled.

We see through rose tinted glasses and love is initially blind. Our brains signal the release of dopamine – the Aphrodite of neurotransmitters and the anticipation of pleasure – to flood the nucleus accumbens – the pleasure centre of our brains. The hippocampus – responsible for memory – records the positive memory of this experience and will recall it when we meet that person again. Add some testosterone, oxytocin and adrenalin to the dopamine and we have a potent love potion. It is all brain chemistry.

Emotions

One man said as soon as women get emotional, he leaves. No wonder he is still single at the age of 56. His interest in women is mainly sexual. Independent, adult, mature, single women do not take him seriously. If he cannot man-up to emotions, he may not be able to man-up in a mature woman's bed.

The majority of men are not in touch with their emotions. Ask a woman to list synonyms for the word "angry" and to arrange them in order of intensity: peeved, annoyed, slightly irritated, indignant, affronted, upset, angry, seething, furious, rage, murderous Medusa. Ask a man to do the same thing. He struggles. He is not language orientated and he is not in touch with his emotions. He cannot name them and often he cannot distinguish between them. Men have three basic emotions. He is happy – which means he is content – it is not champagne cork popping stuff, he is just happy, or he is sad or angry. Often men cannot discern between angry and sad. It is only when a major event really rocks their world that they experience or express intense emotions. Like their favourite sports team winning an international game. That causes elation. A woman they love breaks their trust – they are heartbroken. Someone hurts their children – they are murderous. One man said: "We are not bulletproof, but cowboys do not cry."

Besides the fact that men do not understand their own emotions, they also do not understand a woman's emotions. They tend to react to a situation entirely from their own male perspective and they really find it very difficult to understand it from a woman's point of view, because they are wired differently. Remember, men have cognitive empathy rather than emotional empathy.

> **Case example:** A divorced single mother struggled financially to raise her daughter. Eventually by the time the daughter was 16 years old, the woman had managed to buy a run-down little apartment. She was very proud of her achievement. She had known many hardships, but eventually she succeeded in buying her own place, albeit dilapidated. Her current boyfriend offered to replace her kitchen cupboards. She refused. She explained she experienced his offer as undermining her independence. Kitchen cupboards were too expensive, she could not afford to pay him back and she felt she exploited him if she accepted. The more he insisted, the more aggravated she became that he had no respect for her independence or that he had no inkling of what she endured to achieve it. She accused him of trying to fix her life.

I told her the following story: A mammoth had killed the male hunter. Due to these circumstances, the woman was forced to learn to hunt for herself or perish. She struggled and made many mistakes. Initially she was not strong enough to pull the bowstring, the arrows fell short, the deer ran away. Many a night she was cold and hungry and frustrated, and she cried to the full moon and raised her fist, but she persevered. Gradually she improved and she became adept as a huntress. One day she killed a bison. She danced for joy. She skinned and gutted the animal, preserved the meat in the snow, scraped the skin clean and erected a tent. That night she built a fire and ate her fried meat. She looked at the full moon: "I am a huntress," she shouted, "I did this! I killed the bison and made the fire and I erected my own tent!" She was so proud of herself, she danced a victory dance around her fire. The goddess Artemis was proud of her too. The next day a male hunter came sauntering by. "What's this?" he asked her. "I hunted a bison," she said proudly. He squinted his eyes. "So what," he answered, "what's the big deal? I hunt all the time." "I erected my own tent, look," she said and waved her hand at her little tent. He walked over to the tent and pulled it apart. "That is no way to erect a tent, it will blow over in the first wind." He took the bison skin, picked up her bow and arrows, slung it over his shoulder and said: "Come with me, I will hunt for you. Come live in my tent. It is warm and solid. I will take care of you."

The hunter had no sense or understanding of the woman's pride at her accomplishment, because from a man's perspective, hunting is natural. It made practical sense for him to have her move into his tent. Men cannot feel the same way women feel about situations, because THEY ARE MEN. The boyfriend had no issue with her independence, he just wanted to spoil his woman and be her hero. She understood. A week later the kitchen cupboards were fitted.

Women can often fluctuate between their emotions, without even being classified as bi-polar or having mood swings. Women know what they feel and when they feel it. (Women do not always know why they feel it.) Men do not always know what they feel. It is not that men do not experience feelings, they do. They are just not that tuned into them. They do not know what to do with them and when men cannot figure something out, they ignore it. They hope it goes away. Men have this amazing ability, which I call the Tupperware-syndrome, where they enclose inexplicable emotions in a Tupperware container and place it in the back of the fridge and then they forget all about it. We all know when that lid pops open due to the poisonous gasses that have accumulated in the meantime.

Sometimes they are in love, but it does not fit in with their plans and then they hope it goes away. The sad thing is, if they ignore it long enough, it does go away or it turns sour.

One man described being in love as being "catnipped". Anyone who has witnessed a cat under the influence of catnip will understand. "We can't think in her company, never mind think straight. Our brains don't work. We say silly things, we trip over our feet, and we even giggle. Often, we just stay away from her, hoping it just goes away," he said. "Don't worry," I answered, "most women feel the same, but they will never want to stay away from the man." Tip to the man – Do not stay away!

Different definitions of relationships

A one-night-stand is not a relationship, so I am not discussing it here.

Do all men want sex? Yes. Do all men want just sex or sex all the time? No. Is his first attraction to a woman physical? Usually yes. However, a sexual interest does not guarantee an emotional interest. Sometimes a man's sexual interest can last three months, but his feelings are lagging behind. Initially when men date women they do not have long term plans. He dates her because he would like to sleep with her and perhaps get to know her better. He likes being in her company and it makes him feel good. He does not even know if she will graduate to become the girlfriend, never mind ever becoming the wife. He just likes being with her, now. She smells nice and she smiles.

The complication is that many women only date potential husbands. They do not waste time with guys who do not make the grade. Men can have a good time with women who do not make the grade and they have a completely different tick list when it comes to choosing a wife or a life partner. Sex might attract a man, but it does not necessarily keep him. One man said: "It is easy to get a girl in your bed, it is more difficult to kick her out of your bed." Men usually regard this as a "friends with benefits" arrangement. Very few women can handle "no strings attached" relations.

Although he may not be ready for marriage, he may still be looking for a relationship, for the present, or he is just looking for a good time. Remember the right girl at the right time and at the right place in a man's life, principle.

> **Case example:** A 28-year-old man told me: "I have been seeing this girl for some time now." "What does that mean? Define seeing her?" I asked. "I spend time with her, we hang out, we go places," he said. " Do you see her every weekend?" "Yes," he agreed. "Do you see someone else as well?" I asked. "No, I don't, just her." "Oh. Are you sleeping with her?" I enquired. "Yes," he smiled. "How long have you been seeing her?" I asked. "A couple of months," he answered. "In her mind then, the two of you are in a relationship." "Nope," he shook his head, "I am just

seeing her." I can see all the men turning their hands up and asking "What?" And all the women rolling their eyes and shaking their heads.

To a woman spending time together exclusively and sleeping together equates a relationship. It is not a marriage proposal, but it is a relationship. To a man, it is not. It is only a relationship when he asks her to be his girlfriend and she says yes.

I remind many women that a man is not entitled to boyfriend privileges if he has not formally asked her to be his girlfriend. Men are inclined to take advantage of this situation where she assumes a one-on-one relationship and keeps herself unavailable to others, and he still hunts in many forests. Such men are erring on the side of immaturity – it is the kind of behavior one would expect from a 20-year old, not from a mature man who should respect the emotions of a woman he is sleeping with.

A relationship implies expectations

I asked the men what the difference is between expectations and a challenge. Expectations means he has to work much harder to please her and he has to give up doing things he likes doing and he loses the things that currently make him happy, without gaining anything. Expectations are detrimental to his current status quo. A challenge implies there is an anticipation of a reward. Winning her over is going to enrich his life or make his life easier. Expectations also activate his current insecurities. If he thinks he would not be able to live up to what she expects from him, he will avoid her. He would rather stay away than disappoint her. Even if that is disappointing to her. If he cannot see her disappointment, then it will eventually go away – remember the Tupperware-syndrome!

Too serious, too soon

Because men are not in touch with their feelings and they are still just seeing her, they get a big fright when she labels it a relationship or expresses her feelings, especially when she uses the "love" word. By three months of exclusively seeing each other, spending time together and sleeping with each other, she feels she can tell him she loves him. He is hardly getting to know her. When a woman jumps the gun and tells a man she loves him first, she is forcing him to face his feelings (to pop open those Tupperware containers), and he often runs, because it is too soon, or she is depriving him of the opportunity to make the big "love" declaration and she is spoiling his big surprise and the chance of making her happy and being the Hero.

One man said: "The moment she says that she loves me, it's not fun anymore, it becomes work." "Once it is called a relationship, you have to attend family functions with her." "Why does a woman have to be "in" something? Why can't she just be "with" someone? Let it be," said another.

Hero vs. Alpha and Omega

Women tend to think men rejoice at the knowledge that he is the great love of her life and that she would sacrifice anything for him. Tell him too soon, and he runs for his life. Too much responsibility, too many expectations. When dating, a man does not want to be the Alpha and Omega of a woman's life. He does want to be the Hero. She will die for the Alpha and Omega, she will make sacrifices for him, she will climb mountains, swim seas and give up her home, change her job and her own plans for him. (Notice, she is doing all the work for him.) Alternatively, when he is her Hero, she gracefully allows him to do stuff for her and to impress her. (Notice he is now the one taking action.) Because he is the man, he needs to conquer her heart, not the other way around. He wants her to be worthy of his effort, and she should be appreciative. He wants to kill the bull for her. When she is killing the bull, she is not very attractive. He will kill the bull for the woman he really loves, but not for every woman. It is tiring. "For you I kill the bull, for your sister, I kill you," said one famous man.

I am not telling women to play hard to get, I am only stating that men tell me they are hunters. They want to feel the prize was worth the hunt. However, men do not like to explore a forest set with traps. A woman set upon "being in a relationship" with no other interest in her life, is trapping a man. Real life is not a Jane Austen novel – not in men's books.

Men are wired to hunt

When a man encounters something new, he is curious. His senses alert him. He sees her, he smells her, he hears her, and he wants to touch her.

Now several processes are set in motion. His brain experiences a dopamine secretion. Dopamine is called the pleasure hormone – I dub her Aphrodite. Aphrodite promises pleasure – her allure lies in the anticipation of pleasure and in the addiction to the promise. Anticipation is extended when the hunt is prolonged by unexpected twists and turns, when he cannot always control the events, when he has to think on his feet and exert his skills to capture her. His testes release testosterone – which I dub Achilles – and it primes him for the hunt. It affects his risk-taking abilities, his mood, his lean-muscle mass, it makes him walk taller, talk deeper, his muscles gleam and it makes his coat shine. He becomes a man with a purpose. Testosterone also spikes his sexual fantasies and he has a target in focus. Aphrodite and Achilles work in unison when the hunt is on. The third character to enter the stage is the hormone adrenalin – the cheetahs. When hunting, he will have to move swiftly. He needs oxygen in his blood. Adrenalin works fast to provide the fuel needed for the hunt, but just as a cheetah can only run full speed for 20 seconds, adrenalin is a short-term solution for providing fuel, it only lasts a few minutes in the blood stream. The adrenal glands which secrete the adrenalin, then release the wild dogs, called cortisol. Cortisol also stimulates dopamine and binds with the endorphins – the feel-good hormones, or dolphins – which dull all sense of pain. The hunt seems glorious to the primed hunter.

Alluring Aphrodite promising pleasure; virile warrior Achilles flexing his muscles and swinging his sword; lean, mean cheetah bristling with excitement to chase; a pack of wild dogs baying and yanking at the chains to be let loose in their fury; and playful happy dolphins frolicking in the waves. Imagine this wonderful fountain of thrilling hormones flooding his body, readying him for action, like a naked Greek athlete crouching in the starting blocks at Olympia. He anticipates the hunt and the more interesting the hunt, the more he appreciates the reward. He has to feel he has earned it. How disappointed he must feel and what a let-down, when all this energy and anticipation is wasted when he runs a league or two and is then already presented with the winning laurels! It is just too easy.

This is exactly what happens when a woman succumbs to a man too soon. She robs him of the hunt. He might linger a little for the sexual pleasure, but soon enough a new challenge will lure him away. Or he may linger much longer, purely for the sexual pleasure and because he is too comfortable or too lazy to hunt, but his heart is not in it.

Do not underestimate the interactive neurotransmitters in men, for it motivates them into action. They are wired and pre-programmed to hunt, and they want the reward to be worth the effort. The more unexpected and unpredictable the rewards, the more dopamine is released, the more he becomes addicted to the chase.

This chase can exist even when couples have been married for 40 years. A woman who understands this hunting instinct, will never bore her man. Once they become firm life partners, she can inspire him and accompany him on other hunts. I know a famous geologist, who travels the world, searching for the most interesting phenomena, with his wife at his side, supporting his quest. He actually solved the riddle of the Sphinx, proving it was much older than originally estimated, by analysing the water erosion marks on its backside. This dates the origin of the Sphinx to about 7000 – 5000 BC and not during Khafre's reign circa 2500 BC. This geologist dedicates his life's work to his wife. What a beautiful real-life example of how inspiration can work when the Hero finds his Muse.

Do your own thing. Don't wait

Let us draw an analogy between "doing your own thing" and a woman on a chariot. When she meets the man, she can rein those horses in for a short while. It is fine if the horses prance on the spot, it may even be sexy, but if she halts them altogether and she dismounts, and the horses start grazing and grow fat and lazy... where is the attraction in that? Letting them prance for a moment or two and then setting off again, keeps it interesting. He can race to catch up, he may grab the reins and change their direction to follow his, or meet up again later, but waiting for a man is to allow the horses to grow fat and lazy. Men find it boring and predictable and they grow complacent. The moment she is no longer there, he may begin looking for her again. Or he may not.

As men can grow bored when women's horses grow fat and lazy, so women can also grow tired or even bored if men prolong the hunt or she may just meet another more interesting hunter along the way. Perhaps women should actually stop waiting for men to catch them and rather focus on all the interesting topics, events and issues in their own lives. One of South Africa's famous actors once told me: "I wish I could just meet an interesting woman, who has a passion for something. There are many very beautiful women in the world, there are very few interesting women." He did meet an interesting woman shortly after, and she happened to be beautiful too.

Be independent, it is attractive

Men prefer it when a woman does her own thing because it means she does not expect him to entertain her and give up the things he likes doing. Or he does not have to feel guilty about doing his thing. He likes her and he wants to spend time with her but he also wants to keep doing his thing. It is fortunate if they have shared interests, such as cycling together, but it is not a prerequisite. As long as she has her own thing, whatever it is. So basically, men like an independent bunny? Yes. I told you it is not fair.

Does this doing her own thing mean that when he asks her for a date, she should cancel other plans to accommodate him? No. If he promised a buddy he would come round Saturday evening and she wants him to take her to the movies, he will still go to the buddy, because he made those plans first. He values loyalty. He values her being loyal to her friends too, but only if they invited her out before he did. He does not expect her to cancel gym to be with him, because he won't. Not because he does not like her, he does like her. He just cannot allow her to rule or control his life. He will decide when he sees her, even if it is every day, if she is not busy doing her thing. Men do not mind if a woman tells him he cannot see her on a particular day because she has plans, but then she should suggest an alternative date when she is not busy. Else he may interpret a non-committal answer such as: "We can make it some other day..." as a rejection.

Does this situation change when they are committed? I ask the men: If she is reading a book and she is on the last page and he comes in from the garden and calls her to come and see the bird cage he had built for her, does he expect her to put the book down and follow him? "Of course," they answer. Should she? Of course. And when she asks him to do something for her, what is his first answer? "Must I do it now?" I did not say it is fair. Just smile.

Do not ask a man when it is a convenient time for him to do something. It is never convenient. Just ask: "Would you make a plan please. It would make me very happy." And smile. He will make a plan. Remember the urgent-rule.

The dating game

Let me describe a woman's approach to a date: So he asks her out for a date next Saturday evening. The weekend before the date, she embarks on a shopping expedition. She plans to wear her jeans, but she needs a new blouse. So she cruises one of the major shopping centres searching for the perfect blouse. She finds it, but now she needs shoes in a matching colour. She takes another half a day to look for shoes. She finds a pair, but she is not sure if she likes them. At home she hangs the blouse on the closet door so she can see it every night. She works extra hard at Pilates class that week to drop a kilo. Somewhere during the week, she finds time during a lunch hour to return to the shopping centre to get that pair of shoes. They are sold out. She rushes off during the next two days' lunch hours to other shopping centres to find that pair of shoes. She does. She also buys new perfume and lipstick. She remembers to book an appointment at the beauty parlour. She sends a whats-app photo of the blouse to her friend. Friday night she watches DVD's, but she skips the pizza because she does not want to pick up that kilo. On Saturday morning she gets up at 8 am. She goes to the beauty parlour for a bikini, lip, chin and eyebrow wax, because you never know. While she is there, she gets her nails done because they happen to have the perfect colour to match the lipstick. She gets home at 1pm. She eats something light because she is nervous. Her friend comes over and brings her the perfect set of earrings to match the blouse. They research the guy on Facebook, reread all his whats-app text messages and analyse every word. By 4pm she draws a bath and fills it with aromatic bubbles. She shaves her legs. She washes her hair and conditions it and then she soaks in the bath with a green mask on her face, for 10 minutes. Her friend is happily chatting away. She applies body lotion, talcum powder and deodorant. Her friend blow-dries her hair straight. They also try out the new hair straightener. And they paint her toe nails. She irons the jeans and blouse. Her friend does her make-up. She doesn't like it and they rinse it off and start all over again. By 6pm she gets dressed. Her pantyhose rips. Her friend dashes off to the shops to buy a new pair. No-one will notice if she wears torn pantyhose under the jeans, but one never knows ...

We all know what happened to Bridget Jones. She charges her cell phone, checks her handbag for tissues, deodorant, perfume, hair brush, ID, cash and her new lipstick. Her friend kisses her cheek and wishes her good luck. It's 7 pm. She is dressed, slips on the new shoes, and sprays her new perfume ... He arrives 10 minutes late, but he has brought her a bunch of flowers.

The man's approach to the date: He asks her for the date next Saturday. He works during the week. Saturday morning he sleeps late because he had a boys' night out the previous night. He gets up and grabs a coffee. He visits his mate. They work on the bike. They lie on the couch and watch a rerun of the rugby match. They pop a few beers. By 6pm he goes home catches a quick shower, uses the deodorant, combs his hair. He drives to her place, stops at the ATM at the petrol station to draw money. He decides to buy a lotto ticket because he feels lucky. He also buys mints because he forgot to brush his teeth. He spots the condoms, but buys a bunch of chrysanthemums instead.

That is why he is 10 minutes late. "You look pretty" he says, "and you smell nice." She smiles and puts the flowers in a vase.

One of my male friends described his apprehension regarding Valentine's Day. "Many men dread this day," he says. "You make a date with a girl, but she has expectations. She expects you to book some fancy exotic restaurant, or to come up with some original idea like a picnic on Table Mountain or something and you live in another province. Then you have to buy the flowers – not from the convenient store, I know, but flowers are 10 times more expensive on Valentine's Day, and so are the chocolates. And then you remember she is on a diet, so where do you book a restaurant that serves diet food and you skip the chocolates. So do you replace the chocolates with a teddy bear? That may be corny. Then you have to find a card. It is rather embarrassing to a man's ego to stand in front of the greeting cards stand and select the perfect Valentine's card. Usually we just pick the first one we see. Or we send an e-card. Then on the 14th you have to send her a message early in the morning before she sends you one. Then it is the date and you have to dress up and if you happen to work late or get caught in a traffic jam, she does not open the door. It is very stressful to date a girl on Valentine's Day, so many expectations. So most of us just avoid it," he sighs. I answer: "Have you ever considered that the girl sometimes just expects you to turn up with a daisy in your hand and take her to a romantic movie? It is spending time with you that is important to her, not the trimmings. If the girl is more interested in the trimmings, you are dating the wrong girl."

When a woman meets a new man, she daydreams about the first date; what she is going to wear, what she is going to say and how he is going to respond; where they would be going, how he is going to take her hand for the first time... and the daydream ends when he embraces her and kisses her. When a man meets a woman, his fantasy begins with the kiss and rapidly progresses from there to getting her naked in bed.

Be adorable

How can a woman expect a man to adore her, if she is not adorable? The psychologist Carl Jung formulated the concept of archetypes. In any culture or country if we speak about the queen, witch, prince, magician, shape-shifter, king, protector, saboteur, etc, everybody will understand the characteristics we are describing. This is the archetype – an original or prototype. Let us compare the archetypes of a warrior queen, Joan of Arc or Boadicea for instance. A warrior queen out there on the battlefield with a bloodied sword in her hand is powerful, but she is not very pretty. She commands from a top-down position. The knights rally around her, they are inspired by her to fight and they may die for the common cause. The warrior queen is someone to be respected, but not really someone to adore. The goddess on the other hand is also a powerful and wise woman, but she does not fight. She is feminine, she does not command, but the men willingly adore her and lay the flowers at her feet. She is someone they want to live for. Cinderella is neither admired nor adored. She was not even noticed, until she got all dollied up.

A woman who yells like a banshee, who attacks and violently destroys property, who threatens to hurt herself, who battles and moans, sulks and nags, is not very adorable. Neither is one who slumps around in her track suit pants and Crocs all day, or one who allows herself to be a doormat. I ask again, how can a woman expect a man to adore her if she is not being adorable?

The same applies to men. How can she admire him for being the hero if he does not man-up to it? Beer-guzzling, couch-potatoes dressed in faded gym shorts and dirty vests, who never fulfil their promises, are not very heroic either. Neither are grumpy jerks.

Just a hint to the girls. Most men tell me they adore women in dresses. Soft floral print dresses. The actor said he loves it when a dress flounces. And they love sandals with heels. Not necessarily stilettos. Many men are a bit self-conscious when they have to accompany a woman who does a tricky balancing act on extra high heels. She is so focused on not falling flat on her face, she forgets to focus on him and just having a good time. Men like women who look good in their clothes, as long as they are comfortable in those clothes. And they prefer women not to wear underwear or pyjamas with cutesy teddy bears or little hearts printed on them. They are men, not paedophiles. Corporate suits are fine for the office and ultra-low cleavages at the office are inappropriate – it distracts them from their work, and the work is the quest, remember. Corporate suits can be worn with soft blouses and perfume. Stockings are fine for work, but fishnet stockings should only be worn to a fancy-dress party or in the bedroom, not to work unless you mean "business" with the boss. Bush wear is preferred to dresses when out hiking or camping, and again perfume is always intoxicating, as long as she does not drown in it. Capri pants halving your calves, are out!

It is very easy to spot couples on their first Internet dates – the women are all over-dressed!

Sensual is more sexy

A man's sexual sense is sight. What they see usually arouses them. That is why pornography mainly caters for men. A woman's sexual sense is touch. I often advise men, please do not touch what you are looking at (ie the cleavage or butt!) Stroke her neck, hold her hand, give her a hug, play with her hair and if you really want to spoil her, give her a massage.

Women will seduce men more easily if they focus on a man's senses, rather than talking too much. What he sees, smells, tastes and if she touches him, is much, much more intoxicating, than the words she speaks. Men's senses are very deprived in their stuffy air-conditioned offices. Women know the secrets of a massage, hot bubble bath, candle light, velvet chocolate, silk on the skin, back scratch...

I often advise men to take note of the brand of a woman's perfume. Women do not only buy perfume because they like the scent. They also identify with the image of the girl or woman advertising it and the phrases describing it. This should give him an indication of the secret archetype he is dealing with. There is a great difference between women who think of themselves as mysterious and spicy and those who think of themselves as floral and fresh. If men can read the ad of her perfume and use those words in his compliments, she will be amazed at his insight.

Habitats and watering holes

Single men and women often ask me where they can meet the opposite sex. Besides the obvious social media sites, which are quite acceptable these days, people still meet other people through friends. Many start cycling or join gyms, but no one is at their most attractive with sweaty helmet hair or smelling like Hercules after he had slain the lion. Anyway, it takes a long, long time before people in the gym actually talk to each other. Many singles state they do not want to hang around in pubs and clubs to meet people, especially the older generation. I have noticed that men and women differ in their habitats, like animals. Men are nocturnal and hunt at night. Women forage during the day. Many single women seldom venture out alone at night, because it is dangerous. They may go to the movies or dinner at a restaurant in a mall accompanied by other women, but generally they do not like travelling alone in their cars after dark. They go to the malls and flea markets and food markets over the weekend, during daylight hours. When the sun sets and they have no date, they get DVDs and take-aways and snuggle up in their beds with their laptops and tablets.

Guys sleep late on Saturday mornings and then lie on the couch watching sport during the remaining daylight hours. (Those hours when the girls are out there in the malls, in their pretty flouncing dresses). Or the guys visit Outdoor Expos, while the girls go to the Hobby or Design Expos. When the sun sets, the guys shower and get dressed to go out to hunt. (When all the girls are inside watching DVDs or Netflix). When the hunt was unsuccessful, the guys go home and have a barbeque with their mates and get drunk and sleep late on Sunday morning, when the girls are hanging out at the flea markets and the nurseries and the outdoors coffee shops. Get it?

Sometimes they all do go out to music shows or shows or they listen to bands, or they do go to pubs just to socialise a bit. And then they are too shy or too drunk to talk to one another during interval. Get it?

Just a tip to the guys. Pick-up lines are corny. Do not think yours is particularly original. It is still a pick-up line. What would be refreshingly original to most girls is if you just say Hi, tell her you would like to get to know her and invite her for coffee. One man asked me why girls always cover their wickets. I answered if men would stop bowling at the wickets, the girls would stop covering them.

Match making

Women will easily introduce their male friends to female friends hoping to match make. Men will not. They are very reluctant to introduce their female friends to their male friends or acquaintances. There are two reasons. Firstly, men believe they do not need help to find a girlfriend. Secretly, they know they do, but they will never admit it. It is an ego thing. So if they introduce a girl to a guy, they are signaling that he cannot find his own woman. Men do not object too much if their girlfriends or wives set up dates for communal friends, as long as they are not involved in the process and it does not backfire on them. Sometimes they object, but the wife or girlfriend persists. (One of those examples where she is not listening to him.) He probably knows some secret about the male, which he would not want to divulge because he is loyal to his friend. So if he does not think his mate would make a good match for her new best friend, drop the issue and do not ask questions.

The second reason why men do not introduce their female friends to their male friends is a tribal matter – it is primal. A man regards his female friends as members of his tribe. He is responsible for her and protects her. He resents another male moving in on the women in his tribe. Men agree with this. They usually protest that the other male is not in her league. It is not fair to the girl, who can make up her own mind, but it is the way it is. If a girl's male friends tell her that her new boyfriend is an ass, she had better believe them. Due to their hero sense of protection, they usually only have her best interests at heart. She is in the tribe. Men also regard match making as a lose-lose situation. Ultimately, they are going to lose the male or the female friend or both, whether the couple break up or get hitched. Men hate losing anything. They are quite open to their girl buddies introducing them to their female friends, though. They sort of expect it.

Sometimes a man may actually agree to introduce a female friend to a male friend. Then that male usually carries his stamp of approval. They usually refer to such a man as a "smart guy." He won't mind her dating his pal, because he honestly believes the other man will look after her, but woe to the man who messes with his friends.

Men have a code that they are not supposed to date a friend's ex-girlfriend or lover. Girls have such a code too, but girls are less inclined to stick to it. The reason is that it is a status symbol, especially to younger girls, to have boyfriends. They may cheat, steal and borrow to get one. Young men are more comfortable with being single than young women. Mature older people may have a different opinion. Once they get over the initial hurt of the break-up, they would want exes to find happiness. Older people know love and happiness do not come around that easily or that often anymore and one should pursue it, when the real thing presents itself. Therefore, they sincerely wish their friends or exes to be happy – I did say MATURE people.

Best female friends

A man cannot easily discuss his latest romantic interest with his best male friend. He discusses her with his best female friend. Only his best female friend – his female buddy – can interpret and analyse the new girl's behaviours and advise him on what to do next. Only a female friend can alert him to typical female games, manipulations, flirting techniques and pathological behaviour.

Who is this female confidante who shares his inner secrets? Perhaps she is an ex-lover or perhaps she has always remained a platonic friend. Whatever the case, she now holds a key position in his life. Men value loyalty. When they put their lives on the line on the battlefields, they need to know that they can trust their friends – their comrades and allies – therefore they really put a high premium on loyalty. They are as loyal to their female friends. Woe to the new girlfriend who criticises the female buddy, or who experiences and treats her as a romantic threat. Remember, the female friend is in his tribe, and he will protect her. They are "Brothers in Arms", not "Lovers in Arms".

Most new girlfriends do not understand that they probably need the female friend's stamp of approval, before he makes a serious commitment to the girlfriend. Men have wisened up to the fact that friendships endure much longer than romances. Therefore they treasure their female buddies. Usually a man has one serious female confidante and then a few female buddies.

When women fall in love, they tend to neglect their friends and spend most of their time with the new boyfriend. Men do this to a lesser degree. He may not be able to stay away from the new romantic interest at first, but sooner or later, he needs his girl buddy to touch base, catch up and compare notes. Men do not reveal everything to their romantic interests, but they do share almost everything with the girl buddy.

Understandably women may find this girl buddy a threat. I ask these women: "Do you not have a male buddy whom you discuss your boyfriend with?" Of course they do. And their boyfriends may not like this, at all, but we all have to cope and live with it.

The best buddy is the one who visits you in hospital, who helps you move, accompanies you to the vet when you have to put down a beloved pet, drives you home when you had too much to drink, gives you advice on the car or cell phone you should buy, or which flowers suit which occasion, and tells you when you are getting fat. Sometimes they gym together and go for a beer.

There are rules though. It is not fair for buddies to refer too much to "the good ole times" and thereby exclude the newcomer, especially not if the buddies happened to be lovers before. The role of the female buddy is to make the male look good in the eyes of his new girlfriend. A true girl buddy will give the new girlfriend a chance, if she thinks the girlfriend stands a chance of making her male friend happy. If she suspects the new girlfriend is going to harm her male friend – no chance – the claws come out.

Just as men will sincerely protect their female friends and warn her against dating an ass, so they should value the advice of their female buddy re their new girlfriend, who may be a feisty vixen or a "broken-wing" in disguise.

It does happen sometimes, that both genders realise that the best buddy is actually the person they have been in love with all along. Friends for life can become partners for life too.

Territory

Best buddies aside, there is still the matter of territory. It is acceptable for best buddies to hug when they greet each other, but it is not acceptable to hold on to each other. The new romantic interest has a place reserved right next to the man, but she need not cling to him to claim him. Men do not like other men to trespass on their territory either.

One woman recalled sharing an apartment with her boyfriend's sister when they were students. The boyfriend had a key to the abode. One evening she was sitting on the couch in the living room next to the deacon, who had the Bible open on his lap. Her boyfriend came in through the front door. He walked straight up to the deacon, lifted him by his tie and said: "And who the f*** are you." "I am the deacon," said the petrified man. "Oh," replied her boyfriend, replacing the man on the couch and then retreated into her room. The deacon picked up the Bible and fled out the door. "What were you thinking!" she confronted her red-faced boyfriend. "It has to do with territory," he explained. "I don't like any man coming near you, not even a male relative of yours." The friendship with his sister has lasted a lifetime, the relationship with him did not. Years later, she became good friends with his wife though. Women are not lamp posts to be marked with urine as territory. (Some women do the same to men!)

Men do have this sense of territory. Many men who break up with a woman and who clearly no longer want her, still resent a new man on the premises. "Metaphorically speaking, I used to park in the driveway, now I have to park on the pavement, and there is another car in the driveway. I don't like it," said one man. Some men reserve the parking, by just giving her enough attention to keep her feelings going, but they never park the car. They might want to get back to her one day, but now is not the right time; or they think they may still find someone better, but they do not actually want her to move on and they know they cannot expect her to wait. So they just reserve the parking. Ha!

One young man also proposed to his girlfriend. His plan was that he would marry her, but she had to stay on in her brother's home, while he went off to live and work in another town, until he could afford for her to move in with him. "No-go," said the Big Brother, in the man-to-man talk. "You can't reserve my sister like a table in a restaurant and only turn up over weekends and I must fit the bill. If you can't afford her, then you can't marry her." The young man was being dishonourable. He could not claim territory and then ride off into the sunset. Leaving his brother-in-law to pay for the upkeep, would not provide an incentive for him (or her) to really work hard to afford marriage.

Insecurities

Men often say they adore a woman with self-confidence. If she acts confidently, he knows he will be privileged to have her as his girlfriend. She will be a great girlfriend to have. Believe this. Hesitate in any sense, and he smells the fear and runs. Some men say as soon as a woman feels insecure about the relationship or gets needy, she smells differently. Men

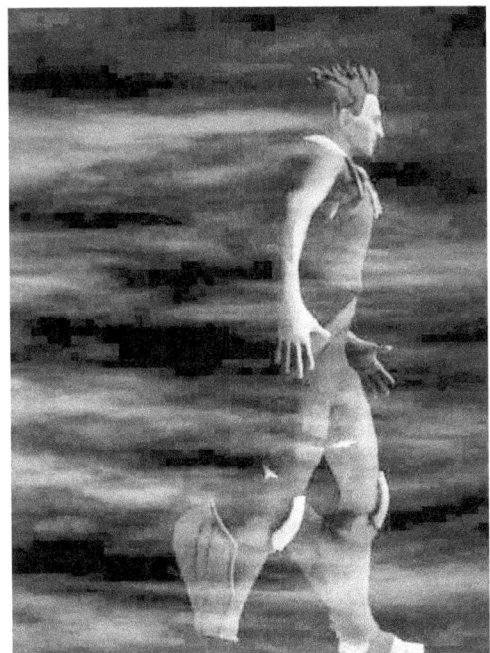 instinctively withdraw when her smell changes. They can smell the fear. One of the biggest mistakes a woman can make is to be scared to lose a man. Once she inhibits her behaviour, or her standards, because she is scared she may lose him, she has lost it. The same apply to men, who are scared to lose the woman. I am not talking about not improving bad habits, I am referring to pretending to be the perfect partner and sacrificing one's own preferences.

It works both ways though.

When a man is insecure and is jealous and overly possessive, he is subconsciously signaling that he does not believe in his own capacity to keep her interest. He projects himself as a weakling and perceives other men as threats and he is not capable of protecting her. If a man feels insecure in the company of other men, it makes the woman feel unsafe. Also, if his aggression elicits a counter attack from other men, she feels even more vulnerable and unprotected. If he is beaten, she becomes prey. Aggressive men are not attractive. Self-confident strong men are. It is fine for a man to know he wants a woman and to show it – it is a sign of confidence. A little possessiveness is fine, a woman prefers others to know they are a couple. Jealous, acting-out behaviour and false accusations are not attractive. Neither are actions such as checking cell phones, opening someone else's mail, usurping emails, cracking passwords, tracking cars and other stalking behaviour. One woman thought it was acceptable to delete all the women on his Facebook friends list. The world population is roughly divided 50-50 between men and women. So take it for granted that your partner is going to cross paths with a member of the opposite sex somewhere, sometime, somehow... Not every encounter between a man and a woman is a sexual encounter or a threat to the relationship. Deal with it.

Insecurities are like shadows on the wall. When we were small, we created shapes with our hands in the candlelight, casting huge monster shadows on the wall. These are metaphors for INSECURITIES. When we trace the origin of the insecurity back to the scared little girl or boy in the corner, we need to take that child on to our lap and tell them what a success we have made of their lives so far. Then the insecurities dissipate. Do not be scared of the shadows on the wall. It is like Don Quixote fighting windmills. Men like women with confidence and vice versa. Women like it when men do things for them, but they do not like men who are too subservient. Too many women are bossy, but deep down they do not like it. I strongly disagree that men should dominate and humiliate women, but women also do not have respect for the men they can boss around. It does not make them feel safe. Neither do the men who bully the women. We will discuss this topic later in more detail.

There is a difference between insecurities and vulnerabilities. We all have vulnerabilities, even men. If a woman has vulnerabilities, it does not necessarily mean she is needy. Insecurity equates to neediness. Vulnerable means she needs a Hero. There is a difference. A man will not expose his vulnerabilities to a woman he distrusts. Men are adamant: If he entrusted the woman with his feelings and secrets, she should not use it against him.

Mens' greatest fear is being a disappointment. When he disappoints a woman, he is guilt ridden. It originates from the little boy not wanting to disappoint his mother. A woman's greatest fear is abandonment. It generates needy behaviour. If her father abandons her, the wolves can devour her. So to men it is often fear of disappointment and the terrible guilt feelings that motivate them to certain inexplicable behaviours and to women it is often the fear of abandonment that drives them to become needy and clingy and manipulative.

The difference between interpreting "No" and rejection, is one's personal level of emotional maturity or emotional insecurity. An emotionally mature person can accept when another person is not attracted to them. It is simply a matter of taste. It may hurt a little, but it is acceptable and one moves on. An emotionally insecure person will interpret the "No thank you" as a rejection. If you are rejection sensitive, get help. Insecure needy women attract Rescuers. The problem is he will never be able to cure her insecurities. He will always try harder to placate her and never succeed, which feeds his fear of disappointment. Eventually they end up as two bitterly unhappy people, who resent and detest each other. Therapy can address insecurities and guide the person to resolve them. No one else can conquer insecurities but you.

Remote control behaviour

Trying to control another person is comparable to holding the television remote in your hand. You can fast forward, rewind, mute and freeze a television screen shot. You cannot remote control another human being. They are humans, not robots. If their feelings are hurt, you cannot fast forward them to "just get over it." Nor can you fast forward them to feel more than they are currently feeling. You cannot rewind and take back the hurtful things you said or did. You cannot mute them by not truly listening or negating their point of view and you cannot mute yourself because you are scared of losing them or alienating them. Perhaps you can adjust your own volume and tone of voice to soften the blow and be considerate. You cannot freeze a relationship to status quo forever. It either has to develop or dissolve. One adult cannot tell or order another adult about what to do. Being together is a voluntary attachment, not an obligation which excludes free will. You can change your own channel, if you wish. Too many people imagine themselves as puppet-masters and are totally amazed when their partners finally revolt.

A last word on dating: When a man truly wants to be with a woman, he will make a plan, even move mountains, to be with her. If he is not with her, then there is a reason for it. A man is quite capable of loving a woman, but not wanting to be with her. This does not make sense to a woman. It can make sense to a man. I did not say it is fair.

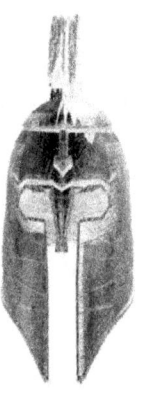

VIRILE HEROES

(I do respect that every adult has the right to decide on moral or religious reasons to abstain from sex and only to practice it within marital boundaries, or not. I am also not advocating pornography or passing any moral judgements. In this section I am mainly discussing the points of view of adult men and women, who date, are married or divorced, without prejudice or intended offence.)

Remember when I said men are an aggressive species? And women need to make peace with that? Well, men are also sexual creatures. And women can make love to that. Or leave. Their testosterone makes them men and their life libido is wired to their virility.

Just to recap on testosterone: The 23rd pair of our chromosomes determine the gender of the child. All fetuses are female originally, unless there is a Y-chromosome, which encourages the gonads to develop into testes instead of ovaries. The testes secrete testosterone, which alters the male's brain and body. I have explained before how this powerful Achilles-hormone primes the male body and mindset for battle.

Much the same happens, when he is primed for sex. They are more apt to risk taking, they think faster, but their judgement is impaired. (In the heat of the moment, men do not consider using condoms or long-term consequences of unwanted pregnancies.) Remember also they reach their sexual peak at about age nineteen, when the nucleus accumbens – the thrill centre of the brain – overrides the neo-cortex, which is the rational part of the brain, considering self-control. By the time he reaches age 30, his testosterone production begins to decline and his risk taking becomes calculated and calibrated according to his physical and mental abilities.

Testosterone also promotes sexual fantasies, but if he is stressed out and ready for battle, the blood supply is rushed to the muscles required for fighting – the arms and thighs. In order for him to obtain and maintain an erection and achieve ejaculation – blood flowing to the phallus – he needs to be relaxed and in the parasympathetic nervous system. Men suffering from long-term stress have a low libido.

When he becomes aroused by what he sees, or what he imagines, the hypothalamus will signal the testes to release testosterone. This release may take several minutes or even hours before the testosterone has an actual effect upon his body, but the effect is powerful throughout the whole body, as testosterone docks in the receptors of almost all the cells in the body. Testosterone cannot be stored. Rivalry increases testosterone and even men watching sporting events have increased levels of testosterone. When a team wins, the fans will have raised testosterone levels and when the team loses, the levels drop. (That is why women should never say: Oh cheer up, it is just a game!).

Interesting facts about testosterone are that in some areas it requires an enzyme called aromatase found in the female oestrogen to activate it. Meat and beer contain oestrogen. Obese men with an elevated number of fat cells, may grow breasts, a syndrome referred to as gynaecomastia, for fat cells carry aromatase. When their testosterone levels drop, men become irritable, tired and depressed – and then they complain women are prone to hormonal mood swings!

On a physiological level men need sex, women do not. Women can live without sex for years. This is not to say they do not enjoy sex or do not want it. Many of them do, but generally they do not need it, in the sense that men need it. Men need it to feel alive, to feel like men. Needing it makes them vulnerable and some women capitalise on this vulnerability. They make the men feel ashamed of the fact that men need sex. Men deeply resent this. It is foul play.

Some women dislike sex, they find it distasteful, painful or just an unpleasant duty. (Please bear with me, I am not referring to women who were molested or raped. That is a completely different, sensitive and tragic topic, which is not within the scope of this book.) I am referring to every day women who just do not like sex. Some of them just do not like their husbands. If you do not like pets, why would you buy one and share your home with one? Men are sexual. If she does not like it, why does she waste her – and his – time by staying with him? "So are you saying if I do not give him sex, I should not be with him?" asked one married woman. "Sex is not something you give. It is something you share. If you do not want to share it with this man, then you should consider why," I answered. "Can't I take a pill to make him appear sexier to me?" she asked. I happened to run into this particular man a year later. He was happily divorced. Other women suffer a temporary lapse in their attraction to their men. When the psychological undercurrent is sorted in therapy, they happily regain their attraction.

Women are definitely not obliged to sleep with every man they date, but it is a vital element in an adult relationship and a marriage, just as emotions are. Reciprocate, initiate, but do not neglect either component.

I once read a bumper sticker where the little stick woman said: No love, no sex. And the little stick man said: No sex, no love. Another slogan said: How can I love you if you won't lie down?

Feelings vs physical attraction

Generally speaking men are quite capable of having casual sexual relations without experiencing any deeper feelings. As one man said: "It helps if you like each other." Women's default mode though, is to get emotionally involved with the men they have sex with. A man may have an intense sexual attraction for a girl, then sleep with her and only then may he fall in love with her. It works the other way around with a woman. Normally she will fall in love with him first, and then sleep with him.

"Why must a girl's feelings get involved?" asked one man. "Would you prefer sleeping with a girl who has no feelings for you at all?" I asked, "then pay a prostitute, or have a life of consecutive one-night stands. Like a perpetual teenager." No one can remote control and fast forward this man to grow up, but he cannot expect a mature woman to be interested in him either. Women have standards. Maybe he will grow into one of those sleazy dirty old men, who pant after young girls. Yuk.

The problem is not that a woman's feelings get involved. The problem arises when she cannot control those feelings. Then she gets jealous and possessive and needy, and her smell changes, remember. Then he runs. With his pants around his ankles, if he has to.

Mature women are quite capable of owning their feelings. It does not necessarily imply that they have all kinds of expectations just because they have feelings. Some women are quite capable of a more relaxed, sex-can-also-be-fun stance. They have lovers. One at a time, for a longer time. They are not demanding permanency, but they do require exclusivity. It is just plain good manners and it has health benefits. Two adult independent people who have a loving relationship and enjoying sex.

A complication also often arises when the man is attracted to the woman and he sleeps with her and then he realises he is in love with her. He retreats because he feels catnipped and out of control. She feels cheated, because she knows he has feelings – women are much better at recognising feelings than men, even men's feelings – but he denies the emotional side, because he cannot afford being in a relationship, for some or other reason in his life – the Tupperware-syndrome again. He did not use her just for sex. He is confused. He needs time out to contemplate what is inside that Tupperware container. But by the time he figures it out she may have moved on when he finally catches on, he actually had feelings for her, or worse she waits patiently and he figures out his feelings are not enough, or she is the right girl at the wrong time.

Just as women should learn to control their feelings, so we can expect men to control their sexual urges. Fair deal? I agree that an over-sexed man whose pants are about to burst is as annoying to a woman as a woman brimming with emotions, is irritating to a man. People are wary of any dam on the brink of breaking. Hysteria rising is not conducive to any relationship. Surely, we can find a compromise somewhere. Many men do actually seek the comfort, emotional growth, back-up trust and friendship of a relationship and many women actually like passionate lovemaking. Surprised?

Despite all the stereotypical jokes that men think about sex every 30 seconds, etc, they do respect women who hold them at bay. Men respect women with standards. There is a difference between a woman with morals who withholds sex initially, and a woman who blames men for wanting sex. Women with standards need not necessarily be prudes, but they are not crude either. Women who value themselves expect exclusivity. After all, would he like to sleep with a woman who sleeps with many different men at the same time?

When a woman gets the idea that a man just wants to use her body for sex, and that he has no consideration for the fact that she is a person, with a brain, a personality, likes, dislikes, interests etc, she feels like a whore. He denigrates her to being an object. At least sex-workers get paid and they know what they are selling. (I have counselled many sex-workers in my practice.)

One man asked why women cannot just regard sex as just another physical activity – like kicking a ball together (!) Here is a little hint: the physical act of sex involves a woman's body being penetrated by the anatomy of another person. It is intrusive and very intimate and very personal. A woman needs to trust the person she allows inside her body. How would this man feel if a virtual stranger whom he has just met or hardly knows, penetrates his body just for fun? It is not just kicking a ball together.

Why would my wife not sleep with me?

Because you may be smelly, drunk or a lazy bum and she is too tired when she goes to bed. Or she is angry with you, because you did something to upset her and you never gave her the chance to tell you about it. If women cannot open their mouths, they are unlikely to open their legs. Or you are boring in bed. Those are usually the women's reasons. Or she is sleeping with someone else because he is paying attention to her. One man observed: "Women are attracted to rich powerful men, because she does not have to fret about a broken washing machine." Point to consider next time it is just too much effort to help her with the chores.

Why would the man not sleep with the woman?

He is getting older and having some impotency problems – which can be attended to by a urologist. He is sleeping with someone else. He thinks she is sleeping with someone else. He thinks she is smelly and drunk or too fat. He does not trust her. He is bored. She cut her hair and wears Capri pants. He is stressed, which would affect his libido – he is also just too tired. Point to consider next time she complains he does not work hard enough to buy a new washing machine.

Make-up sex

When a woman did something to upset the man, and she wants to set things right, she can make love to him and he will forgive her. Making love is an action and men are action orientated. They experience seeking intimacy as a sign of seeking reconciliation. I am not saying that women should manipulate men with sex. If she thinks she can just make love to him, without sincere remorse for what she has done, he will take the sex, but not forgive her. It is foul play. This also depends on the severity of the transgression. Sleeping with him in order for him to forgive her for sleeping with his best friends is not going to work.

If a man messed up and thinks he can make love to the woman as an act of retribution, he is making a BIG mistake. It does not work that way in a woman's world. The woman wants to TALK about it first, before he touches her.

Affection

Most women thrive on affection. They like to cuddle and to be touched. Remember I said a woman's sexual sense is touch. If a man wants sex at night, it may be a good idea to shower her with affection during the day. By the way it is not advisable to touch a woman when she is cooking or nurturing a child. Men often hug their wives when they are standing in front of the stove. Don't. She is tending to the saucepan simmering on a hot plate, her hands smell like onions and she is not feeling sexy. Same applies when she is changing a nappy or feeding a child. She is in Mommy-mode. A man would not like it if she distracts him when he is fixing a sewerage problem and his hands are full of pooh, or when he is holding a power tool in his hands. She will appreciate it if he helps her to prepare dinner, or just chats to her. The sooner the evening chores are done, and if he draws her a bubble bath, well now, that might work. Just to mention it, many men like affection too. People differ in their opinions on a public display of affection. It is just a personal thing, nothing to cause a major raucous about. Just communicate personal preferences!

The cuddle hormone

Everybody knows testosterone is the male hormone and oestrogen is the female hormone. Oxytocin is the "cuddle" hormone. Both genders produce oxytocin during sex. This makes men feel tender towards the woman they are intimate with and it makes them feel vulnerable. Many men realise this. This is often why men grab their pants and run after sex. They know they are vulnerable, and they do not want to share those vulnerabilities with her. She may exploit his vulnerability. Some husbands no longer sleep with their wives, not because they do not want the sex, rather because they are avoiding these vulnerable episodes. He does not trust her with his secrets any longer. Some men abscond right after sex because he knows this is also the time when his feelings for her will surface and he is not ready to face those feelings – just in case she gets the idea that sleeping together means a relationship. Some men cannot deal with her feelings.

The adult, mature thing to do is actually to stay the night. Cuddle her, hold her and make her feel safe. Isn't that what being a hero is all about? Basically, if you are not prepared to stay the night like a gentleman, do not get into her bed. If you are not ready for the relationship, or just interested in casual sex, at least have the decency to honestly discuss this with her before you get into her bed. You may be surprised at her answer. Not all women equate staying the night with "now we are moving in together," but women are not generally in awe of "fly by nights".

What is your number?

I know of women who have had multiple lovers, yet they will never be classified as sluts. They are discreet and classy and very interesting. A person's level of experience does not necessarily correlate with the number of lovers they have had, and neither does their classy-slutty rating. One man put it very eloquently: "I don't care how many previous lovers my current girlfriend had. Whoever crossed her path in her past, contributed in some sense to shape her into the woman she is today and that is the woman I fell in love with." If someone keeps an alphabetical list with ratings and little stars allocated on their bedside table, we may have a problem.

Bad boys

When I interviewed men for the purpose of this book, they often said: "I am not like other men." Then I replied: "What element of manhood do you not want to identify with?" They all answered that they disapprove of men who take sexual advantage of women. Why do men have a bad reputation when it comes to their sexual behaviour? Most men are quite aware of the fact that women get emotionally involved when they have sex. Yet the men prefer to ignore this or hope she won't. So he sleeps with her, because he needs the sex and then he disappears because he wants to avoid the emotions. "A time to come and a time to go, and this is usually five minutes apart," said one man. "Come hell or high water, this cowboy is going to ride tonight," said another bad boy.

Men pursue a woman and when she capitulates and he sleeps with her, he loses interest. This is hurtful. Yes, men do this, rather regularly and they hope they can get away with it.

This kind of behaviour gives men a bad name. This is using the girl for your own carnal pleasure. It is also a very dangerous thing to do with damaged girls, (who are usually the promiscuous girls) but we will discuss that later. The male slut actually has a bad reputation as much as the female version.

I am not denying that there are some people, of both genders, who truly do not mind indiscriminate no-strings-attached-sex. It is just a pity that they sleep with people who do mind. Nobody wants to be just another f***. A woman is not a "take-away" sex shop. It is disrespectful and carries a health risk.

Some men take advantage of drunk girls, some men brag about the girls they have had one-night stands with, and some men tend to tell very crude sexual jokes in the company of women. Women can be quite boisterous when they joke about sex as well and they can take these jokes. Some of these jokes are very funny, but there are limits. If sex is the only thing a man can talk about, if he gropes and goggles all the time, he is being a nuisance. This is the male equivalent of the woman being needy. Nothing wrong with a virile man, it is sexy and attractive, but once it becomes a desperate preoccupation, it is boring.

One man had sex with his girlfriend and half an hour later he broke up with her. He told her he came over with the intention of breaking up, but she looked sexy, so he decided to have sex one last time!

Pornography

(I am not discussing the topic of child pornography or other illegal activities in this book. Please refer to one of my other books on crime. I am also not entering into a discussion about the morality of pornography. I am discussing adult men's views on the topic.)

> **Case study:** One young lady of 19 years caught her boyfriend watching pornography on his laptop. She was bitterly upset. In the ensuing (one-sided) argument, she raised the fear that since she was a virgin before they slept together, perhaps her love making was inadequate, and that he compared the bodies of the porn-models to hers. Her self-esteem crashed. He was mortified and felt like a pervert. She expected him to promise to never-ever watch pornography again.

Most of the men who read this case study, just shook their heads. "If she wants him to promise never to watch porn, she should promise him never to have a bad mood during PMS," said one. "But PMS is a biological female function she has no control over," I answered. "So is watching porn to a man, it's a biological need," he answered.

Most men grow up watching pornography, since their teenage years. A man's sexual sense is visual. That is why there is such a major pornography industry catering 99% to male viewers. They also masturbate since their teenage years and naturally turn to pornography as visual stimulation. Teenage girls masturbate too, by the way. Teenagers watch pornography because they are curious about sex and the female or male bodies. Teenage boys are brimming with hormones and curiosity. Sexual prowess, virility and experience are benchmarks of manhood and just as they compete on sports fields, they compete in this as well. It is part of being a man. Young men masturbate much more than young women do. They may even masturbate in the shower, right after they had sex with their girlfriends, just because they are aroused by the warm water, or the memory of what just happened. The poor young woman may jump to the conclusion that she was "not good enough." "Just join him in the shower, sweetheart," advise the older men.

As men grow older and mature, their interest in pornography may wane. They may watch it once a week, once a month or just every now and again. I asked them what the main reasons would be and they answered: "Just because I am bored." "There is no current woman available, ie girlfriend." "To relieve stress." "Because I am a man and I can." "Sometimes I watch it with my girlfriend." "To check out a new technique." "My girlfriend refuses to give me oral sex, so I watch it on porn." "If women expect men to stop fantasising about sex, then women should stop daydreaming about romance."

Women generally object to pornography because they regard it as an exploitation of the female body and everything associated with that topic; because they feel their own bodies compare inadequately with those of the porn models' and because they regard it as cheating.

Most of the men concur that they do not compare the bodies of the porn models and actresses with the bodies of their wives and girlfriends. Given the choice of whom they would rather make love to, they all answer they desire their girlfriends and wives. "My wife is a real person. If I have sex with a porn model, I might as well have sex with a blow-up doll. She is not real. My wife does not act in bed. Her enjoyment is real. That is a real turn-on to me." "Only an insecure girl would be jealous of the body of a porn model and insecurity is a major turn-off. It is the same as a woman only wanting to make love in the dark. I want to see her. My body is not perfect either, but it provides me with much pleasure. Hopefully she feels the same about her body," said another.

The men also concur that watching pornography is not cheating. "Watching porn is a natural male activity, it actually has nothing to do with her. I do it in private and she should respect my privacy regarding this. If I wanted to cheat on her, I would break up with her." Most men also advise that a woman should be grateful her man rather watches pornography, than seeking relief from a sex-worker or having an affair.

Some women like watching pornography with their partners and the general consensus among men is that they appreciate this. Not every time, but now and then it can offer variety and spice. Usually they may start watching a pornography DVD and then really get into their partners to the extent that they completely forget about the DVD.

How would one determine if a man is addicted to pornography?

Generally, in psychology the definition of an addiction or fetish is when a person prefers this activity to having normal sexual contact with another adult. In other words, if a man prefers watching pornography to actually having sex with his partner.

Other indications of an addiction are when a person spends an unusual amount of time and money on an activity, to the extent that it interferes with their daily functioning and leads to financial debt. When watching and collecting pornography supersedes any other interests, sports and hobbies, we may have a problem. Continuously watching pornography may also lead to increasing curiosity and desiring more devious sexual practices. Adult mature men know the boundaries and they can distinguish between fantasy and reality.

Last word on pornography: Generally, women would prefer men do not watch pornography. Generally, men would prefer women not to have periods. Live with it.

Advice to the 19-year-old girl: Don't lose your man because he is a man.

Impotency

As men mature, their virility is still very important to them, but they realise their health is important too. Women are not so concerned if he fails to rise to the occasion in bed now and then. It may be mortifying to men, but it is not to the women. Women know what it feels like to be too tired. Anyway, there are other ways to make her happy or just cuddle. What would raise her concern is when the state of his general health or his negligence in taking care of himself, is the cause of his lack of libido. If he does not manage his stress levels it can lead to ulcers, diabetes, heart attacks or strokes. That is very serious to her.

When the mind or body is under stress, it releases the cheetahs – adrenalin – to produce glucose as fuel. However, adrenalin is a short-term solution. If the stressful events are prolonged and severe, the adrenals release the wild dogs – cortisol. Cortisol is a catabolic steroid, which counters the effects of the anabolic steroid testosterone and it inhibits the production of sperm. Like a pack of greedy, hungry wild dogs, it attacks the body in its crazed need for fuel. It converts muscles into amino acids, breaks glycogen down into glucose and fat cells into free fatty acids. Whereas it will at first increase arousal, it will soon enough attack the immune system and cause an all systems break-down.

Libido is not just a sexual energy. It is an elixir.

Quite often men downplay serious health issues due to their egos. They refuse to visit psychologists, urologists, cardiologists and neurologists. Don't be stupid! Would you want your wife to be obstinate and refuse to visit an oncologist when she has been diagnosed with breast cancer?

 Read more about: CORTISOL THE DEATHLY STRESS HORMONE on page 171

Attraction

It is true that men are initially physically attracted to what they see. However, they also agree a sustainable relationship does not depend solely upon physical appearance. A woman too preoccupied with her own body and beauty will lose her man as she is paying too much attention to her body and not to him.

On the other hand, a woman who neglects her own body is also not attractive, for she may neglect him too. It is true that most men are not attracted to overweight girls, but most of them are also reasonable. They do not all expect the women to look like models. They are not that concerned with every blemish or centimeter of cellulite, as long as there is fun in bed. Remember the actor who said there are many beautiful girls but very few interesting girls.

Men do not want to be embarrassed by the women at their side, just as women want to be proud of their heroes.

The stereotypical "men are just interested in a woman's looks", is as false as the saying that women are just interested in a man's money.

Some very affluent men also happen to be very interesting, intelligent and sexy and it may just be these attributes that attract interesting women to them, and not just their money. It may be that their determination, shrewd business sense, hard work, ethics, wit and strategic thinking that enabled them to make that money, also make them attractive to like-minded women. Some people attach a high premium to physical looks, others attach more value to materialism and others appreciate intellect or humor. Attraction is idiosyncratic. So is sexual chemistry. Overweight women with panache and confidence may not be as beautiful as their skinny superficial sisters, but they are often more attractive. (By the way, not all skinny, beautiful girls are superficial.)

Last word on the virile Hero:

One man explained to me how he feels when he makes love to his wife. "I am standing in front of her, stripped of my armour, naked with only my manhood to defend my honour. I am vulnerable. She can castrate and destroy me in an instant with a look or a word. I take the risk because I desire her. And I desire that she desires me, as I desire her. I need to see it in her eyes, feel it in her touch, on her breath, her voice, the essence of her body. If she reciprocates my desire, I feel nurtured, invigorated and my energy is regenerated. I am a man. I will do anything for her, grant her every wish and I will protect her. When I feel loved, as expressed by the physical act of love, I open up and I want to talk to her, share with her and dream with her.

Making love to the woman you love, is not just a physical act. It is a spiritual experience, giving meaning to manhood." Wow.

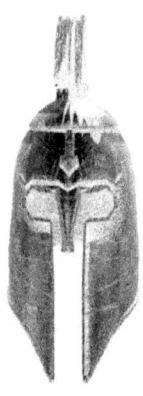

ROGUES, VILLAINS AND VIXENS: PATHOLOGICAL RELATIONSHIPS

Anybody wanting to read about serial killers, stalkers, rapists, child molesters, paedophiles, and women who kill can refer to my other books. In this section I would like to discuss the despicable antics men and women get up to in everyday relationships, often breaking the law, but getting away with it.

Rogues

Let us discuss the annoying bad behaviour first before we get to the serious stuff. Most wives more or less have the same standard complaints about husbands:

Major complaint: When a woman asks a man to do something for her, he forgets, postpones, does it grudgingly or just does not do it. Did she ask nicely? Most women say they do ask nicely the first time. Not so nicely the third time. Men are always busy with something more important. Filing the taxes, calculating the family budget or preparing litigation due for court the following day, is important. Completing a computer game is not. She is your wife. You committed to doing things you do not want to do. Man-up. You would expect her to interrupt her television programme if you needed her attention. So please, when she asks nicely, just get up and do it for her. I am asking nicely.

Serious complaint: Men talk to their wives as if they are stupid. They are impatient and grumpy and condescending. They seem to justify the reasoning that because they are tired, they are entitled to be grumpy, patronising or just plain rude. Is there then the understanding that she can refuse sex because she is too tired? Or because she dislikes making love to a grumpy old wretch. He considered her to have a brain when he asked her to marry him, so why would he insult her intelligence now? This is especially bad when men belittle or patronise their wives in company. Nobody thinks he is the hero for talking to her like that, quite the contrary. "You are the anti-hero. Did you learn to be bitchy from your mother?"

Men don't help in the home. If both work, both help. Get up, man-up.

Many men use women just for sex. True. Many women use sex as a weapon. Also true.

Men cheat – so do women. Men lie – so do women. Men drink – so do women. Men yell – so do women. Men abuse drugs – so do women.

Husbands' general complaints about wives' bad behaviour is that they nag, sulk, flirt with other men, check up on their men unnecessarily, become needy, bitchy, bossy, talk in THAT TONE OF VOICE, tell them what to do and they withhold sex.

From bad to pathological, the incredulous stuff

Certain human emotions lead to dangerous pathological behaviour. Rejection sensitive, insecure, overly dependent, immature, angry, jealous and possessive people are damaged. Damaged people are dangerous. Remember, one cannot expect rational behaviour from an irrational mind. I repeat: Damaged people are dangerous. You cannot fix them. A chemical imbalance in the brain cannot be loved away. They need professional help.

Abusive men

Some men are born with a remote control in their hands instead of a rattle. They honestly still believe that due to their anatomical gender they are ordained to lord it over their women. I met a man who told me he was upset that his girlfriend dared to talk to other people at a dance, without his permission. No girl had ever done that to him before, he assured me. She had to keep eye contact with him when they went out for dinner and if her eyes strayed, he would call her a whore. His inferiority complex actually marched into a room ahead of him and announced him. She asked me if I thought there was something wrong with him. Run, baby, run. Some women tend to think if she loves him enough, he may change. If he does not love himself enough to be a true hero, then your love is not enough, sweetheart.

Some men tend to think that if they are right, everybody else is wrong. Again, recall my example if the world was filled with billions of clones of YOU, it would be a very boring place. These men insist on arguing and raising their voices, until everybody else in the company finally keeps quiet. They are not keeping quiet because they agree with you, they are keeping quiet because they realise the absolute futility of talking to you. Go home.

Even other men regard these men as obnoxious jerks. The jerks then fall victim to the "betrayal" syndrome. His friends did not betray him, they left because they had enough of an arrogant know-it-all twit. This is often also the same guy whose girlfriend left him "in his darkest hour" which should read "his foulest mood."

The above are usually also the men who feel they can only solve a disagreement or get people to do what they want them to do, by threats and violence. Men are aggressive by nature, but if they cannot control their tempers, they are in the same league as those emotionally out of control women who cut their wrists every time they do not get what they want. These men are usually cowards among true heroes. Violence, cruelty and bullying are not characteristic of a true hero. Men do not have to be macho tough to be heroes.

Feisty vixens

Some women have the notion that to throw objects at men, break things, scratch cars, break windows, damage his clothes, burn his books, etc. is feisty behaviour. It is not feisty, it is not cute, and it is not sexy. It is tacky behaviour and it is unlawful.

Just for the record so is breaking and entering, climbing over walls and fences and forcing doors open, even if she did share the house before. So is opening someone's mail, hacking into their emails, downloading secret tracker devices on phones and cars without the owner's permission, diverting their calls and messages, and publishing defamatory comments on Facebook. Demanding someone's attention and actually using violence or force or a weapon such as a tazer gun to enforce it, is unlawful. Pointing a firearm, firing a firearm in a built-up area, and keeping an unlicensed firearm is unlawful. Biting, scratching, hitting, slapping and pushing someone around is assault and unlawful. Chasing someone with a car is unlawful. Restricting a person's movements and holding them hostage or locking them up in a place against their will is unlawful. Stealing a car or taking property that does not belong to you, is unlawful. "Donating" his clothes to charity without his permission, is unlawful. Lying under oath and making false accusations is unlawful. Contravening a protection order is unlawful. Now you know. Just in case anyone thought it was acceptable to do this, or that they could get away with it forever. I wish more people would actually prosecute.

Anything one posts on Facebook and Twitter and other social media is considered published and one can be sued for libel, racism, hate speech, etc, which are all unlawful. Even if you just like or repost someone else's defamatory remark, you can be prosecuted. People do have a right to privacy. Do not publish or tag their photos without their permission.

Literally sending hundreds of SMS', missed calls, messages and whats-apps is obsessive compulsive behaviour. It is a mental disorder. Calling a current or ex-boyfriend's new girlfriend, his friends, parents, family members, boss and colleagues and spreading defamatory libel is unlawful. Turning up uninvited or "coincidently" at places he frequents, following him and sitting in a parked car outside his residence or turning up and causing havoc at his place of work or home can constitute harassment and stalking behaviour. Stalking and harassing someone is unlawful. This means there are laws against it. One can be sentenced to jail for several years for it.

Checking his phone, emails and rifling through his cupboards is sneaky. If he wants her to know something, he will tell her. Or she can just ask him. If he trusts her and opens his life to her, he will voluntarily share his Facebook profile with her, probably tell her where he goes and whom he meets. Even happily married couples have a right to freedom of movement and privacy. They voluntarily share information, they are not obliged to. Respecting privacy does not necessarily imply keeping secrets from each other.

The above examples are all behaviour I have observed and encountered, executed by women – supposedly normal girls whom men date. This is what one man refers to as his girlfriend "going mental".

I have also encountered similar behaviour from men, but then I need to add the one incident where the man set the woman's house on fire. That is unlawful too.

I do not deny that anger, pain and anguish are very real emotions, but no matter what the intensity of those emotions, is does not justify acting-out unlawful behaviour. You are not above the law. Get therapy please, or you may just get a sentence.

The Rescuer

I have referred to the Rescuer, earlier. Some men confuse being a Hero with the archetype of the Rescuer. They always walk into the trap and feel the need to rescue dependent, oversensitive, emotionally unstable women. These are often the women who slice at their arms when the men walk out. These women need to be treated "sensitively" because they have emotional troubles. Eventually their emotional oversensitivity consumes the man, who ends up counting his words and walking on egg shells, in case he upsets her. These are often the men who are motivated by those deep-seated guilt complexes.

The oversensitive, "damsel in distress" adopts a victim mode and gets secondary gain from the man's "handle her with gloves" behaviour. The man reinforces the victim mode. If he does not pay attention to her, dance to her fiddle and compensate for her "sensitivity", she pouts, sulks, scolds, bites, withdraws and punishes him relentlessly in several ways. In such a manner she skillfully manipulates him into becoming her puppet, catering to her every emotional whim. She alienates and isolates him from his friends and family. The moment he indicates he needs a breather and time-out with his friends, she creates some drama he has to attend to. She has absolutely no tolerance for his female buddy and often issues an ultimatum to him in this regard.

Sometimes insecure men prefer to rescue these "broken wing" women, because these men find normal, stable, mature women a threat to their own fragile egos. Some men I interviewed immediately recognise this female behaviour as pathetic manipulation tactics.

"No matter if you turn left or right, it would always be the wrong choice," said a recovered ex-Rescuer, "I always felt as if I was in trouble, no matter what." Another man described this relationship as a Big Black Hole. "She remains the centre of this hole and you just get sucked into the nothingness, losing yourself completely."

The Greek hero Thesseus entered the labyrinth at Knossos to find and slay the Minotaur, but his love, the princess Ariadne, gave him a ball of string to guide his way out. Unlike Thesseus, the Rescuer eventually becomes a mouse in a maze who can never find his way out. Unlike Ariadne, who aided her lover, this victim-woman finds pleasure in placing obstacles in his path. Where there was a path yesterday, and he ventures there today, she has moved a thorny bush in his way. He may buy her roses because he knows they are her favourite flowers, but when he buys them again, he gets berated for spending too much money. There is no order, no pattern, no route, but he desperately tries to figure it out, against the odds. "You need to fight for me," she calls, but at some stage a tournament is won, and the victor is rewarded with the lady's scarf. Not the poor Rescuer lost in the labyrinth. He will never reach the epicentre of the labyrinth and be rewarded the peace and tranquility one is supposed to find in a mature relationship. Eventually he sinks down and covers his face for he can no longer face the futility of the madness of trying to please her. Hopefully he has friends who can rescue him, or a good therapist. Remember the sayings: If you want to feel good, then you have to let go of bad feelings," and "you cannot start a new chapter if you keep on reading the last chapter." To save himself, a Rescuer HAS TO LET GO. Don't just walk away... run like hell.

There is a neuro-psychological theory explaining the Rescuer-Victim duet. The hypothalamus in the brain produces chemicals (peptides) which match our emotions such as anger, sadness, victimization, lust etc. and our bodies respond in a pre-programmed manner to these chemicals. When we become addicted to these emotions, or states of being, we will subconsciously attract someone or something to the brain cell which gratifies the bio-chemical craving of the cell. A woman with victim-mode peptides will always attract a situation that would gratify their sense of being the victim. The Rescuer will always be drawn to the "damsel in distress" for it fulfils his brain's biological craving to rescue. If one cannot change one's emotional state, one is addicted to it. Breaking an addiction requires effort, and you cannot expect your life to change, if you are not prepared and willing to make the change.

> **Case example:** He meets her in a bar. She is quite sexy and has a certain vulnerability about her. Perhaps she had a tad too much to drink. Clearly, she needs protection. He takes her home – his home. She is not that drunk, he finds

out, when she seduces him. It is wild sex. He can hardly believe his luck. The next morning, he offers to take her home. (She has already sussed out his car, wrist watch and his abode. "I can live here", she thinks). She is currently crashing at a friend's place, because she recently lost her job, because her boss was sexually harassing her, so she resigned. "Don't worry," she says, "I will find a place to stay and a job." He calls her later, fantasizing about that wild sex. She does not take his call. She went for a job interview, she tells him later. As a bar lady. It's not ideal, she explains, and her house mate is kicking her out and she needs the work to get her own place. "It is not ideal at all," he answers, "why don't you move in with me in the mean time? I will take care of you." Gotcha.

Our parents warned us: Do not pick up stray cats. They have fleas, they stay in our homes and fall pregnant and it is very difficult to get rid of them.

Victim-women have more staying power than super glue. They are master manipulators. At first she rewards him with great sex for rescuing her. Then she starts becoming extremely pathologically possessive and jealous and he has to report his every move to her. It is a major catastrophe when she cannot get hold of him immediately and then like an AK47 rifle set on automatic rapid fire, she blasts him with hundreds of SMS messages per minute. She scowls every time he responds to someone else's SMS and she scrutinises his phone to check who called. She checks his whats-app sign-on times and compares them to sign-on and sign-off times of perceived female rivals. She tries her very best to get hold of his cell phone and deciphers his passwords. She keeps tabs on his car's mileage and intercepts his bank statements and cell phone records. She consumes him and drains him, but he becomes addicted to the crazy sex. "These women f*** as if it is the last time in their lives. It is wild, but also desperate and there are no deeper feelings involved," said one recovering Rescuer. In some sad, sad cases, there is not even any sex at all.

Subconsciously some men are attracted to such a narcissistic woman, because it provides a welcome alternative to the women who usually make him the nucleus of their existence. If it is all about her, then he can be the Hero, fulfilling her needs. That makes him feel good, and wow, the sex is good. However, that narcissism needs to be constantly fed, and she feeds on him. The narcissism actually camouflages a deep-seated dependency and desperate neediness.

There is another neuro-psychological theory explaining the seemingly narcissistic behaviour of the damsel in distress / victim, who is solely focused on having all her needs gratified and shows no empathy for the suffering Rescuer. The anterior cingulate cortex of our brains integrates cognitive and emotional information. It assists us with interpreting emotional signals from other people – it is the emotional intelligence part – and it activates our fear of rejection. When it is damaged, it reduces our expression of empathy.

Another part of the brain involved in directing the behaviour of the damsel in distress is the amygdala. Emotional instability and cognitive impulsiveness are behavioural manifestations of the amygdala, which reacts severely to negative stimuli. The amygdala attaches severe negative emotions to memory. A lack of serotonin in the frontal cortex inhibits the amygdala and impairs the ability to evaluate, integrate and act on cues from the environment. It also prevents both the Rescuer and the damsel in distress from ceasing responding to unhealthy stimuli and returning to healthy stimuli.

There is a psychological phenomenon called disorganised attachment style, characterised by ambivalent behaviour. As children, these women were probably emotionally impoverished, which can literally cause an increase in the size of the amygdala. When the dopamine levels in the amygdala fluctuate, it causes the extreme fear of rejection, which leads to totally irrational behaviour. "I will love her more and promise never to leave her," he reasons, but no amount of love can cure a chemical imbalance in the brain.

I ask these men their opinions about women who return to abusive men who hit them. "They are crazy to go back, it is ridiculous and makes no sense for them to go back," is the general consensus. "Then how come you return to the woman who emotionally abuses you?" I ask. "Somehow, the moment I am with her again and I hold her in my arms, I immediately forget all the hurtful things she has done to me," states one Rescuer. Oxytocin, the powerful cuddle hormone, inhibits some memory consolidation and increases positive social memory. This may be the reason why we forget and forgive the hurtful things done to us by people we love. Oxytocin overrides the rational neo-cortex warning us. The trick is in not going back at all and to avoid that situation where the oxytocin is released.

In an experiment involving rats, every time the rat presses a lever, he gets a food pellet. However, if the dispenser completely stops giving the rat a pellet, he becomes despondent and gives up completely. When he is randomly rewarded with a pellet, he becomes almost addicted to pressing that lever. When the damsel in distress rewards the Rescuer now and again with a smile or approval, he becomes addicted to her and keeps on trying harder and harder to please her, despite not getting a "pellet" most of the time.

These women have serious abandonment issues. Sooner rather than later, he realises he is trapped, and his life energy is being sapped and he wants to get out. Instinctively she recognises the alarm signals, and she grows more tentacles. Often she falls pregnant to trap him or she already has a child or two to string along. I know of one woman who has four different children with four different fathers and still the men do not catch on. Such a woman falls pregnant deliberately in an attempt to tie him to her. The moment he makes it quite clear that he has no intention of marrying her, or when he insists on a paternity test, she aborts the fetus. Some of these women have the baby, purely to have a lifelong hold and connection with the man. They will callously use the child to play on his guilt complex and to bleed him dry with maintenance. FOR EVER.

The men are just too scared to tell her outright to leave, because then the women "go mental." The men feel like anti-heroes for "hurting her feelings". These Rescuers then try to justify their situations by convincing themselves that the women truly need them and that it is not that bad. It is that bad. As a matter of fact, it is worse. Then they try the bad behaviour tactic, hoping she would break up with him. Forget it. She won't. She will just make your life more miserable. In the meantime, he is still getting the incredible sex, and she gets all cuddly and cute afterwards (when the oxytocin is flowing). Then he wakes up in the middle of the night to find her downloading all the info on his phone and transferring his computer data to hers and she sends rude and nasty messages to his ex-girlfriends and his female buddy under his name.

When he confronts her she cuts her wrists, because she "loves him so much and she can't stand the thought of living without him." She makes him promise he will not leave her and then banks on the knowledge that he would despise himself if he breaks his word, for the sad thing is, the Rescuers are often honourable men. Terribly misguided, but honourable.

When she cuts her wrists, or "freaks out", please take her to hospital and since she is out of your house, pack her stuff, change the locks and leave her stuff with the friend she stayed with originally. Go to hospital and tell her. She cannot commit suicide in a hospital. Inform her therapist. Also tell her you are going on vacation, you will not be at home and you are not going to take her calls. Go to a safe place, alert a security company to look after your house, alert your friends, and DON'T TAKE HER CALLS or respond to the messages. When such people are rejected, their egos react by turning up the volume. If you can resist this turned up volume and just sit it out, they will eventually tire and turn their attentions to someone else.

Advice regarding that stray cat: Put the cat out. She will meow and growl and scratch at your door and try to sneak in when you leave a window open, but eventually she will leave and don't worry, some other sucker will take her home.

They are locked in a deadly dance, until he breaks away. Breaking an addiction implies a period of extreme withdrawal symptoms, but eventually he will form new neuropaths and alternative behaviour, develop a sense of self-worth, and attract a woman with self-worth.

I agree that these women need help. Professional help. Some of them, however, visit psychologists not for the purpose of healing and coming to terms with their hurt, but only as an added bonus to elicit sympathy. Men would be advised not to get involved with these women, but to wait until she completes therapy. A professional therapist may guide her to reach a point of forgiveness, healing and maturity, where she has gained insight into her manipulative behaviour, learnt that she cannot control another human being with her own disturbed emotions, learnt to love herself, and where she is prepared to give and receive freely, without scorn.

We all encounter emotional obstacles in life, in one way or another. No one is exempt from pain, loneliness, heartbreak, betrayal, loss, rejection, abandonment, ridicule or trauma in various forms and intensities. To the women who recognise themselves in the above scenarios, please get professional help. Find a therapist who will attend to your pain, who will walk the road with you, who will guide you to find your own true north and help you to liberate yourself from unrealistic expectations, who will develop your insight into your own manipulative behaviour. Manipulative behaviour holds no true benefit for you. A good therapist will assist you in finding the core and becoming the stable, mature woman you were meant to be. Would you not rather one day want a man who stays with you willingly, because you are adorable?

And to the Rescuers out there, please do not waste your valuable heroism in a bottomless pit.

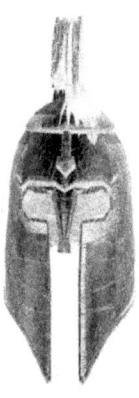

HEROES GETTING HITCHED

Imagine a group of nine-year-old boys having the following conversation: "So what colour suit are you going to be wearing at your wedding one day? Have you designed it yet?" "Would you like lilies or roses in your bouquet?" "Did you know that you can get fairy shaped glitter confetti?" IT DOES NOT HAPPEN. Boys do not fantasize about their wedding days or marriage. Not when they are little and not when they are grown up either. Marriage is a serious responsibility and it fits into a life plan at a certain stage in their lives.

When a man gets married, he makes a promise to the woman he has chosen, that he will protect her and provide for her – and their children – for as long as he lives. I repeat: this is serious stuff. He is taking on the responsibility for her financial, emotional and physical wellbeing, for the rest of their lives. Therefore, if he is not yet capable of the financial, emotional or physical means to take on this enormous task, he is NOT READY. "But I will work too and with our combined salaries we can make it, and we can rent a cheap apartment and share a car, or we can stay with my parents..." whine the starry-eyed young girls. "And there you go, sweetheart, telling him what to do, and planning his life for him, which is exactly the reason why he does not want to get married," I answer them. "But I just want to be with him," they sigh. "And what can you offer him?" I ask.

I remind the girls of the Jane Austen novels. In order to get married, a woman had to be accomplished. She needed to be proficient in playing the piano-forte, singing, dancing, letter writing, prose and poetry, embroidery, bookkeeping and running a large household with an army of employees. Many things have changed since the Victorian era, but the fact that a man requires certain "accomplishments" in his wife, has not. He is not going to marry a woman just for her looks.

Men seek different qualities in a woman they marry than in the girls they date. One man told me when choosing a long-term life partner a man looks for a woman with class, (classy, not sexy) she must be presentable, intelligent and original. A wife has to have dignity. She wears the crown as his queen. His friends must approve of her. (His girl buddy too.) A man wants to be proud of his wife. He has a certain benchmark for the appearance, level of education, knowledge, image and inner qualities that he searches for in a wife. It is an idiosyncratic choice for every man.

Another said: "My life partner must have my back when things go bad. I need to feel safe with her, I can trust her. She supports me. She gets my quest. She is financially responsible." When I asked him what he meant by having his back, he answered: "It's not just in the big things, but also in the smaller things. She won't divulge my secrets or vulnerabilities. If I go to bed at 7pm some nights because I am just dog tired, she won't mind or tell anybody. If I am self-conscious about my stomach, she keeps it a secret and buys me health food without making a fuss about it. She does not tease me about my baldness. She does not make a fool of me in public. Many women think it's funny to tell quirks about their men at dinner parties. It is actually deeply embarrassing. If she has my back in the small things, she has my back in the bigger things too. When things go bad, I need to know I can count on her to stay positive, to support me, not blame me and not leave me."

Many of the very wealthy men I spoke to told me they are acutely aware that they can lose their fortunes in a flash. Circumstances change and the world economy is precarious. Making money involves high risk taking behaviour. This makes them vulnerable. (Not insecure). They need wives who can understand this, without taking advantage of their deep-seated vulnerabilities, wives who will stick to them, even if they lose the money and wives who will trust them to come up trumps once again.

It often happens that wives' intuition warns them regarding some of their husbands' business deals or business partners. Unfortunately, then the man perceives his wife's warning as criticism. Please view her as a resource in your camp, with your best interest at heart, watching your back and scanning the grass for snakes. She is good at this. Heed her instinct. She is your wife and your ally, not your enemy.

Let us take an in depth look at men's so-called fear of commitment

A wise man explained the difference between being committed and being involved. "If we have a breakfast of bacon and eggs," he said, "the chicken was involved, but the pig was committed." That is why men are so scared of commitment.

One man explained it as follows: "When you get married it means you are willingly entering into a contract with another person, which entails you are going to have to do things you don't feel like doing, every single day for the rest of your life. Those are the expectations. For that kind of commitment, you want a reward. It needs to be worthwhile." "What about being with the woman you love, about making love, laughing together and not being lonely," I asked. "Is that a reward?" "No" he said. "I can just live with her or just have a relationship with her and still get all of that." "Then what is the reward?" I asked. "The reward is knowing she has my best interest at heart, knowing she adds value to my life, she has my back and I am safe with her. Also, every man wants to protect his woman, and to know she really needs me. She also needs to know what I am giving up for her." "Is she not giving something up for you?" "No. She is gaining security. I am losing my freedom."

Sometimes a man just fears committing to the wrong woman.

Expectations again

Another man explained expectations: "Expectations are like overtime at work; the first time you do it, it is appreciated, the second time it is expected. When you woo a woman, you take her out weekly, when you marry her, she expects it." Many men have told me they resent the fact that the wives are no longer the girls they dated, because wives expect more. Perhaps the husbands are no longer the men they dated either? Becoming a husband actually entails giving up bachelorhood.

One man said men only get married and settle down because they enjoy the comfort of it. Someone tends to them. Their laundry is sorted, there are groceries in the cupboard and food on the table. Of course, he conceded, the husband does his part too. He checks her car's tyres, mows the lawn and such. Marriage is purely the dual comfort zone that a relationship moves into. "Also, when you date, you have to work hard. When you are married you can let go a little and you are off the hook. You know she won't leave if you relax. A girlfriend may just leave if you grow lax." So marriage is the space where we can all grow fat and lax?

What I noticed about men's description of marriage is the almost absolute lack of mention of romance. Men need seduction, women need romance. Maintain the balance and we have a win-win situation. One man advised: "Keep him lusting for you and he will provide the romance."

Why do some men marry brainless chicks?

When a man asks a woman to marry him, he is acknowledging that he respects her intelligence and independent autonomous ability to make one of the most important decisions of her adult life. Yet some men tend to think the moment he puts that ring on her finger, somehow it causes a lobotomy to her cerebral cortex and she is incapable of making decisions, or not even worthy of having an opinion on the decisions he makes for her? Some men really treat their wives as brainless chattel. Some men assume the moment he marries her, he inherits a right to condescending behaviour.

The majority of men concur they dislike a yes-and-amen girl who agrees with him all the time, yet the moment she differs from him and voices her opinion, he calls her opinionated? Men explain they like a woman who voices her own opinion as long as it is not done vociferously and as long as she can still acknowledge his point of view and does not tell him he is wrong. He is still going to act on his conviction. When she continuously differs from him on every single topic, he begins to wonder if they have anything in common and whether it is time to move on. Then she is opinionated.

A mature woman does not expect her husband or partner to report his every move to her. However, it would be considerate of him if he communicates his movements to her, just as he would appreciate her informing him of her whereabouts. It is not checking up or restricting, it is called communication and caring. If he behaves secretively, he may be the one sowing seeds of suspicion. Just tell her.

Marriage is a partnership where both parties do things they do not feel like doing every day. When they were single, they could skip doing the dishes now and then, go to bed at 7pm if they were really tired, feed the dog from the plate or wear jocks two days in a row. When married they have to consider another person sharing a very intimate space. Sometimes it is fine in a marriage just to say: "I don't feel like cooking tonight." And it is wonderful if the partner says: "That is ok, we will just get take-aways." Sometimes it is fine to say: "Can we do the dishes tomorrow morning, let's just go to bed early tonight." Two adults can compromise and accommodate each other. But things change once they have children. You cannot say: "Let's just skip bathing the baby tonight and go to bed early." Manning-up to the task, walking the extra mile and really committing to doing something you do not feel like doing, increases tenfold when there are children, but apparently the rewards are ten times better too. So they say.

A man has a plan

Men are much more pragmatic than romantic when it comes to marriage. Men also think and plan much further ahead than what women give them credit for. Men just do not always tell women about these plans. They first want to see if the plans work out and surprise her, rather than disappoint her when they do not achieve what they had planned. The majority of men have a plan – many plans.

> **Case example:** Our engineer finally landed a job in Dubai. Very excitedly, he informed his girlfriend. She was happy for him, but not elated. He asked her what was wrong.

111

"What about us?" she asked. "You are coming along of course," he answered. "Arab countries do not allow men and women to live together, you know this," she said. "You are coming along as my wife then." "I am not going to marry you under these circumstances," she said. He left. Later he asked her again why she would not marry him. "You only want to marry me because it is convenient for you and it is unlawful to live together." "No," he answered, "I planned to ask you to marry me anyway in a year's time when I had saved up enough money. Getting the job in Dubai, just brought it forward. It is more practical this way." She had no idea that he had plans to marry her. She said yes.

What do women want?

Many men ask me what women want and I have mentioned it before. Women WANT TO BE SAFE and they want attention. Once their basic needs such as a roof over their heads, food, clothes and retirement etc are fulfilled, then they prefer their husband's attention rather than the gifts he buys her.

Case example: A man called me and asked my advice on how to save his marriage. From Monday to Friday afternoons he would stay in a small bachelor pad in a city close to his company's headquarters. His wife and children stayed in another city in their mansion. He would Skype his family every night. Friday afternoons he commuted home. He arrived home exhausted and preferred retiring to bed early. He conceded that he was rather grumpy on a Friday night. Saturday mornings he slept late. Then he spent the rest of the day with the family. Saturday evening he took his wife to a fancy restaurant. Sunday was a lazy day and they would take the children to a family restaurant or visit friends or family. Monday morning he returned to the other city. Once every two months he treated his wife and children to a game lodge long weekend. He also took them abroad every December on a ski vacation. He said he only got sex during the lodge weekends or when he took her abroad. He felt his wife was only giving him sex when he spoilt her with a vacation. His wife drove a fancy car and she did not need to work. His wife was having an affair. He could not understand why. He felt he was really working very hard to provide for his family and to keep them in luxury.

I asked him if it would be fair to keep a dog locked up in the court yard and once every two months take it out for a long walk in the park. Dogs need to be walked every day, even just for 10 minutes. Else they dig a hole under the fence and go visit the neighbour.

One night, when the husband was out of town, the home alarm went off. The neighbour came out and assisted and tended to the wife – who was dressed in her nightdress. She made him coffee. He became someone she could talk to. If a woman cannot talk to a man, it does not take her long to find someone else she can talk to, and so on.

She enjoyed sex with her husband on the lodge weekends or vacations for those where the times when she felt connected to him, when she had his attention. She experienced it as a duty just to please his needs on weekends and that is why she resented it. He was not there during the week nights to lock the doors, check that the alarm was switched on, hold her and make her feel safe. His marriage did not last. Both misunderstood the other. She felt he neglected her, and he felt she was also not in tune with his quest. She was not prepared to support him and fulfil her part of the bargain by raising the kids, while he worked hard to provide a luxurious life style. Marriage is a complicated commitment. It is not just white satin and confetti.

If it is important to her

Women do not expect men to understand all their feelings, but they do expect men to respect these feelings. I repeat, women are emotional creatures. So, if it is important to her, it should be important to the man, even if it is not logical. EVEN IF IT IS ILLOGICAL.

> **Case example:** A young couple have a baby. They are both exhausted. Saturday afternoons they play with the baby. He suggests that one of them takes a nap while the other

plays with the baby and then they swap. This way they can both get some rest and the baby is not unattended. She said no, she wants both of them to play with the baby, because she misses him and wants to spend time with him.

In this case he was being pragmatic, she was being emotional. There is no right or wrong. It is a male-female thing.

Case example: A woman was involved in a legal dispute with a man. It was settled, but the whole affair left her upset and feeling vulnerable. Later she found out that her dentist husband had taken on this man and his wife as his patients. She felt her husband was disloyal regarding her feelings about this couple. He had a pragmatic approach and said business was business and the legal dispute had been resolved years ago, so she should "get over it." He was not taking her feelings into consideration, and she felt betrayed.

Case example: A young couple moved into their first home. In the back yard there was a jasmine creeper that had overgrown the patio, obscuring the light from the kitchen window. One of the reasons why she loved the new house was because of the jasmine, but she agreed it was out of hand and they would welcome sunlight in the kitchen. One Saturday afternoon they were both pruning the jasmine. She was happily snipping away twig by twig, until she noticed he had cut off two of the three main roots at ground level. The brand new marriage of six months almost ended in a divorce right there. His reasoning was it would take ages to prune the plant and if he cut it at the root, it would grow again. He knew it could take years to grow, but it was their first house and they planned to live there for years. Her reasoning was if he could not respect her feelings about the plant and trying to preserve it, how would he respect her feelings about more important issues in the marriage? Her attachment to the plant was not logical, but it was important to her. Metaphorically men

114

can sometimes just walk all over women's flower gardens with their big feet and not understand why her feelings are hurt. Gently guys, tread gently.

A final word on marriage. I know a woman who was married to her husband for almost 40 years. He was a keen yachtsman. Every weekend they spent at a local resort, sailing his yacht. They retired to a seaside town where he was a member of the local yacht club. Many vacations they spent sailing the seven seas. Literally. They chartered yachts in the Greek isles, the Caribbean, etc. Occasionally they went on safaris with the 4x4 utility vehicle. After his demise I went to visit her. She was planning a 4x4 holiday. "Why don't you go sailing?" I asked. "I don't like sailing much," she answered. "You have sailed most of your life with your husband. How can you say you don't really like sailing?" Her comment left me flabbergasted, but her answer was even more incredible: "He loved sailing," she said misty eyed. "It made him happy." Now THAT I call love.

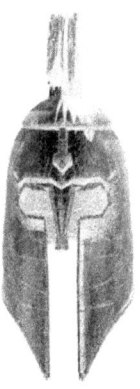

THE ANTI-HERO:
BREAK-UP AND DIVORCE

Do not kick the bunny

Remember when I said no-one kicks the bunny? Remember when I said
men hate to be the anti-hero? Men tend to stay with women, not because
they like her or want to be with her, but rather because leaving her
would imply kicking the bunny. And that makes him feel like the anti-
hero. So he is trapped in a no-win situation. He yearns for his freedom
on the one hand, but he weighs this up against being the anti-hero. Being
the anti-hero is worse than staying in a bad relationship. So he stays.

Often he convinces himself it is not so bad. Often he just shuts up. He feels guilty if he disagrees with her. One man told me he stays in his 30-year unhappy marriage for if he divorces, his children and friends would find out about his affairs and that would make him an anti-hero.

Men often start behaving badly, hoping she will break up with him. Now he mistreats her, acting like an anti-hero. Then he feels guilty about his despicable behaviour and he does something nice to relieve his guilt feelings – not due to any feelings he has for her. It is about HIM feeling better about himself, not about making HER feel better. She unfortunately sees this act of goodwill as hope for the relationship, so she desperately clings on. He tries to break up, she cries, he takes her back. Not because he wants her, but because he hates being the anti-hero who kicked the bunny. And she sleeps with him.

In effect this woman is keeping the man attached to her by manipulative emotional blackmail and sex. We can try to fence a dog in, but the moment we give him a gap, he will make a run for it. If he does not stay on the veranda willingly without a fence, he does not want to be there. Does a woman not rather want a man to stay with her willingly, because he wants to be there, because he adores her, rather than he stays because she manipulates him? So the man begins behaving badly, hoping the woman will kick him out. Remember men don't talk, they do. They seldom say: "I want to break up." They behave badly, so the women will say the words. Kick him out ladies, he is begging for it.

To the men staying on in such relationships, due to some misguided sense of obligation or guilt, I ask: "Would you want a woman to stay with you if she does not want to be there? Would you want to be one of those guys who keep women tied to them by threats and fear? Of course not. So why do you allow her to keep you tied to her by manipulation?" Go.

Cheaters

Some men cheat and have affairs. Some men hope their wives will forgive them. I asked the men how they would prefer their wives to react when they find out that the men were sleeping around. Except for the one man who said he would like it if his wife joined him and his girlfriend, most of the others concluded that the wife should not feel threatened about him sleeping around. "It is usually just sex," one explained. "I would not want to sacrifice the stability of my family life for the girl I am sleeping around with." A man may be sexually turned on, but emotionally turned off.

Men seem to distinguish between "just sleeping around" and having an affair. An affair is more serious and involves emotions and can be a threat to the marriage. I asked the men how they would react if their wives were having affairs. Unanimously they agreed that they would take it seriously, because "women's emotions are involved when they sleep with a man." Do they ever consider the emotions of those women they are just sleeping around with?

Many men cheat. Some people say it is in a man's nature to want to "sow his seed." Some men may cheat, but then he meets one woman whom he will never cheat. He loves her, he does not want to hurt her, and she fulfils him emotionally and sexually. She is the ONE he stays true to.

Let us explore a woman's typical reaction to her husband cheating on her. Her reaction is basically the same to any lie.

I explain to men a woman's intuition (that little alarm that tells her when something is wrong – when something threatens her safety – for that is all that intuition is) is as deep seated as a man's aversion to being the anti-hero. That scares a man. For he knows that awful, devastating, debilitating feeling of being a disappointment, being the anti-hero. It is unbearable. The difference between men and women is, when he is the anti-hero, it drains his energy and debilitates him. The hero's battery is flat. On the other hand, when women feel insecure, they get active. Their minds go into turbo mode and they tell themselves all kinds of nasty things and then they act on those nasty things. They check his phone, hack into his emails and laptop, open his mail, track his car, follow him and hire a detective. They phone people, threaten people and sometimes they even poison people. I kid you not.

> **Case example:** I listened to one man describing his wife's paranoid jealousy and possessiveness. I asked him why he did not obtain a divorce. He said it would crush them both financially. His wife and children were beneficiaries of a trust and it would be a very difficult process to extract his

finances intact. This raised the alarm for me. "So your wife would gain more by your death than by a divorce. Are you sure she is not poisoning you?" He assured me she would not go that far. A week later he came to see me. His face was ash white. His domestic helper had confirmed to him that the wife had asked her to procure muti (poisonous plant material) to poison him. He moved into the garden apartment on his property and only ate meals he prepared himself.

This man did not cheat on his wife, but some men do. Men often hide the truth from women because they want to "protect" them. Believe me, she knows already, or she suspects, and a suspicious, insecure woman is a dangerous woman. TELL HER. If a man cheated on a woman, he thinks he can hide it from her. She knows. Deep down, she knows, because her intuition warned her. Some women may prefer to ignore it, because she is not strong enough to confront it, or she may believe she cannot live without him and she does not want to lose him at any cost, or she may not want to sacrifice the lifestyle they share, or she protects the children. Or she had an affair herself.

Tell her everything

Most women, however, will go into detective mode, find the facts and confront him. Most men initially try to deny it. This is futile. By the time she actually confronts him, she has the evidence. She asks him to tell her everything. Men do not tell women everything, because they fear her reaction. He knows she will explode, and he will be the anti-hero. So he tests the water, by telling her a little, just to see what her reaction is. Then she finds out something else, or she already knows something else. That is when she will explode.

> **Case study:** A wife confronted her husband with his philandering. She invited him to tell her everything and promised that they could continue the marriage. He confessed. She forgave him. Later she found out that he failed to mention that he came on to his best friend's girlfriend. When she confronted him in a fury for keeping

this from her, his answer was: "It didn't count, because she said no." She did not forgive him again.

The fact that the man is lying to the woman makes her angrier than the fact that he slept with someone else. Sleeping with someone else is a major betrayal, and excruciatingly painful to her, but she may just forgive him. He will be in the dog box for a long time, but remember women put the highest premium on the love of their lives, so she may forgive him and be willing to try again. However, if he lies to her, he is negating her feminine intuition. He is making her doubt her own safety alarm. Her safety alarm is a primitive primal mechanism. It overrules love – remember Maslow's hierarchy of needs. If he threatens her safety in this manner, she turns animal. Now she goes for the jugular. She goes for the money, because it makes her feel safe and she knows she is hurting one of the heroic elements – provider. If she hurts him financially, if she makes him pay for her hurt and the emotional threat and humiliation of losing her safety and security, she is stripping the hero of his armour in public. She does not want him to be in a position to be the provider and hero for another woman. Few women are rational when it comes to divorce settlements. They do not consider their actual expenses, they want to be compensated for the emotional hurt. They feel entitled to his money (manhood), because he rejected her womanhood.

Bitter witches

When a woman divorces, she not only loses her man. She loses her protector. Now she becomes a single woman. She becomes prey to predators. She is not safe when she drives her car alone at night, mechanics and handymen are going to take advantage of her, she has to cultivate a new set of friends, couples no longer invite her for the wives fear she will steal their husbands, and the husbands fear she will lead their wives into temptation. She has to attend to her own financial affairs and learn new skills, she has to trust strange men, fight her own battles and heaven forbid, she may even have to work. This makes her feel unsafe and she will make him pay for it.

When women divorce, some of them lose their providers too. These women develop an indignant, self-righteous entitlement to his money. "I deserve more than what is offered in the divorce settlement, because I kept his house and raised his kids and sacrificed my own career for him," they argue. These are the same women who employed au pairs and nannies, who enjoyed the privileged lifestyles of manicures and tinted eyebrows and weekly hair dresser appointments, who spruced up their tans on exotic beaches and skied in the Alps, who drove fancy little German sports cars, who never smiled at their husbands, always had headaches and basically bored their husbands into a divorce. Now she is out to financially ruin him? I said it is not fair.

Women regard divorce as losing their security. Men regard it as gaining their freedom, eventually. But first they go through hell.

Man-down

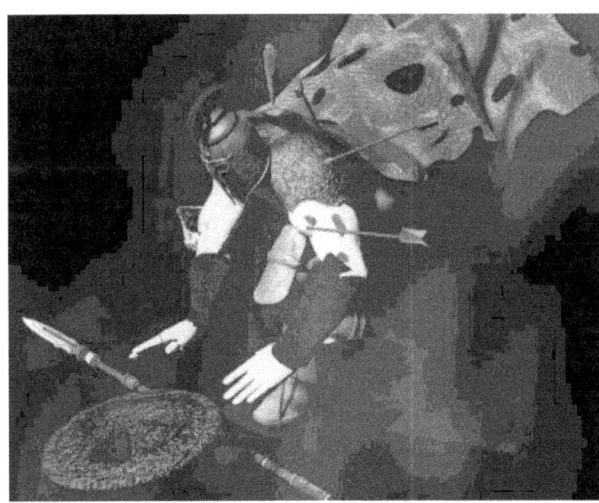

Few women realise the absolute hell men endure when they divorce. I have walked this road with some of them and believe me, it is ugly. It reminds me of the aftermath of a battlefield. Women see their heroes going off to war in their shining armour, full of bravado. Women do not walk the aftermath of a battlefield. It is carnage. Men put up a brave face when they divorce. For a week or so they have a sense of bravado, realising that freedom is a viable reality sometime in the future, but soon enough they retreat into their caves. As a therapist I have been privileged to be allowed into this man-cave. Initially just as the silent witness to their pain, and then slowly, gently to remind them of the lost hero inside them and to guide them to find it.

I have seen men remain in marriages with women who will just never ever be happy no matter his effort. Men stay, because it is the right thing to do. He suffers in silence, he pays his dues and he does not cheat on her. He stays despite her total narcissistic, deep seated, sullen unhappiness. He stays because good men do. Then one day, he says: "Enough."

Cave mode, phase one: He walks out of the marriage, straight into the cave. No matter how much of a calculating, manipulating, scheming shrew she was, he blames himself for failing. For not trying harder to meet her standards, no matter that she kept moving the goal posts. He blames himself for leaving and walking out and being the anti-hero. He paid her a generous settlement, he gave her a house, he pays maintenance and yet he stills feels like a failure. For three months he cannot even lift his head and look people in the eye. These men seek therapy and just sit and sob. They excuse themselves from work because they cannot cry in front of their colleagues or personnel and they sit on my couch and they just cry and cry and cry. They feel embarrassed, but they also feel safe with a therapist. Then they mumble a thank you, and they snatch their keys and they go home and take a sleeping pill. Two days later they are back on the couch and they sob. Because they failed. As providers. It was just too hard. Like a field nurse in a war zone, the therapist sees them emotionally naked, stripped of their hero armour, vulnerable and bleeding. Part of the healing process is for the man to admit that he is bleeding and to cry, because it hurts.

Phase two: Then they get angry. They need to re-establish themselves as men who are not ruled and controlled by women. This is when they fire their secretaries, cut their adult daughters' allowances and some may go on the rebound and seek hard core sex. Contrary to popular myth, most of them do not seek hard core sex, because their libidos are depleted and they know it will only exacerbate the anti-hero feeling. They know indiscriminate hard-core sex will actually make them feel worse. However, some do go out with the boys and for some reason the boys think it is a good idea to get the men drunk and then they may allow themselves to be seduced by a woman who throws herself at them. They usually feel ashamed once they sober up and will avoid her at all costs.

(Pity the poor woman who thinks a man in this state is a good catch and that he will stay with her.)

Phase three: Then he retreats deeper into the cave for he has disappointed himself again. He is a bad man, he thinks. Disappointment and guilt are bedfellows, remember. The continuous calls and SMS' and whats-apps from his ex-wife, hell-bent on revenge, just confirm his disappointment in himself. He may be drinking too much, or sleeping too much and missing work, which exacerbates his low self-esteem. So there he sits in his cave. Smelly, consuming copious amounts of alcohol laced with self-pity, which erupts into a physical and emotional hangover, feeling at his lowest ebb.

Then one day, just like at the end of his marriage, he says: "Enough." He gets up, stretches, takes a shower and walks to the edge of the cave. There is a world out there and he actually misses being a part of it.

Phase four: He exits the cave and he gets active again. This could be about a year after the divorce, or later. At this stage he avoids all women and fraternises with men. Suddenly he attends gym and enters an iron man competition. He needs the testosterone to restore his depleted male reserve. Male bonding makes him a man among men once again. Then he may date here and there. Not because he is actively seeking female company, but usually because his friends' girlfriends or wives set him up. He agrees to the date because maybe he could score sex. He would prefer just the sex with no emotional ties and the sooner the woman shows any emotion or any expectation of long-term possibilities, makes any demands, tells him what to do or expects him to report to her – he is off like a lightning bolt. He seldom progresses beyond a second or third date. He becomes one of those guys who doesn't call. This makes him feel bad. Coming up with excuses or avoiding her calls, also makes him feel bad. This triggers the anti-hero button. So he stops dating.

During this phase men begin working very hard again. Work makes men feel good about themselves. It is an action. He feels competent. Like the proverbial Phoenix, his self-confidence is slowly rising, but it is fragile.

Phase five: Establishing himself as a male by working and working out may last about another year. We have now progressed two years. He has recovered in a sense from the financial blow of the divorce and adjusted his financial status. Perhaps not to where it was, perhaps better, but it stabilises. He might find a new place to stay and move out of his buddy's garden apartment. He lives on his own, because he may not acknowledge it to anyone, not even to himself, but he is sort of going to need a place to bring a girl home to. He justifies this by saying he needs his own space.

Phase six: He is happier at work, he is fit and he is living in his own place. He has the ex reasonably under control. He does not suffer an anxiety attack every time her name features on his cell phone or in his inbox. (He has dubbed her The Complainant.) He has learnt to cook. He is tired of socialising with his single buddies, because they drink too much and he finds it meaningless. There must be more to life than that. His other buddies are doing exciting and interesting stuff with their girlfriends and they get sex. He does not get sex and he does not do exciting stuff, like spending weekends away at a resort. He actually realises he is a bit lonely. He misses the camaraderie that a marriage is supposed to bring. He would not mind seeing a girl, perhaps a girlfriend. Just for a while. As long as she does not get serious, or bossy, or expects him to report to her. So he starts dating again, discerningly.

Phase seven: Then one day, he meets a woman. He falls in love. So does she. He gets lots of sex. He is all over her. He is "catnipped". He loves pursuing her, feeling like the hunter, like a man. He loves being someone's hero again. He makes her laugh and they make love. She responds to his extensive attention and she assumes this is a relationship that may lead to something more permanent. And she mentions the L word... and he runs like hell. Back to the cave.

Phase eight: So he is back in the cave. He digs up all the pain of The Complainant. Because loving her brought him pain and admitting he actually may love the new woman, leads him to remind himself that he can get hurt and become the anti-hero again. So he sits in the cave reminding himself why it is a bad idea to be with the new woman he has fallen in love with. He hopes if he avoids her and keeps busy, the feeling of being in love will go away.

Meantime, the wise girl will not follow him into the cave. I asked a man what a woman should do when a man retreats into his cave. He said if she retreats and becomes distant herself, he will experience her as unreliable or tell himself that he was right to leave her because she is not interested anyway. If she follows him into the cave, she is needy and persistent and an insecure stalker. He will just retreat deeper into the cave or attack her. If she keeps herself busy doing nice exciting things, but he is not invited, she may revive his interest, depending on his level of healing and maturity.

Where he sits there in the shadow of his cave, he can see her dancing among the butterflies in the sun. If he is ready and healed, he will come out and join her. If he is not healed and still attached to the pain of the previous relationship (I say attached to the pain, not necessarily attached to the woman who caused it) he will watch the new woman, but not join her and tell himself she deserves someone better. He may lose her, he may even lose the love of his life, but we have already been through that discussion. Hopefully he will man-up and take her, because at this stage of his life he should realise that the right woman, who has also been tempered by life, might just be the best thing that can ever happen to him. It may just be the right woman at the right time, but he is so scared to take the plunge and risk it. He missed out on the love of his life before, does he really want to do it the second time? You do the math. Last chance at happiness, Odysseus, wake up, nobody is perfect.

Getting back to the process of divorce: Seldom do both parties agree to a divorce simultaneously. Usually one party wants a divorce and the other does not. They may benefit from marriage-termination therapy. Few people realise divorce implies an emotional divorce, a financial divorce and a lifestyle divorce.

Emotional divorce implies that the person you relied on is no longer there. The person feels betrayed, angry, sad, lost and perhaps hopeless. This may lead to vindictive, desperate and irrational behaviour. (One woman removed the light bulbs every time the father spent the weekend with the children in the house. He retaliated by disconnecting the geyser.) Years later, people are embarrassed about how they acted out during a divorce. Many women remain emotionally dependent on their ex-husbands. They still expect him to come to the rescue when they encounter problems and many women actually create problems to force the men to come to the rescue. They still expect him to come and help when the car breaks down. (Call the AA). Some men remain emotionally dependent on their ex-wives and need her approval on every major decision he makes. Part of the emotional divorce is to learn to cope on an emotionally independent level, to deal with the loneliness and to find new meaning in life, cultivate new friendships and eventually to re-establish and redefine a different relationship with the ex, especially if there are children involved. It also implies establishing some sort of relationship with the ex's new partners, respectively.

Financial divorce implies maintenance, setting up trusts, changing wills, transferring ownership of cars, title deeds, selling and buying properties and disentangling often enmeshed financial arrangements. Divorce usually means a lowering in the living standards of all involved. Financial implications also imply some of the women who were dependent on their husbands, now have to learn to manage their own finances and retirement portfolios. It may imply setting up her own medical aid, car and house insurance, bank accounts, etc. This may be daunting at first, but ultimately liberating too. It may also imply returning to or entering the job market.

Lifestyle divorce implies breaking up the home and resettling the various parties into new homes. It is sad to lose communal friends and the in-laws, who may have become cherished during the marriage. Making new friends and socialising is often hard work and difficult. Separate single vacations and negotiating Christmas and New Year's alone are milestones.

Pets may be lost and missed. Learning to make decisions on your own, without consulting a partner, but also without needing the approval of a partner can be frightening, but also a relief. Even the simple daily routine of waking up and finding there is no one to share coffee with, is a major adjustment. BUT people do survive this, and they get over it, and they move on with their lives and they do find happiness or at least new meaning in their lives.

Suffer the little children

Many men do not want to walk out of unhappy marriages because of their children. I have often explained to them the best Dad is a happy Dad. Children adapt. No person is left unscathed by a divorce, but neither do the children who grow up in marriages full of strife and spite. I have met children who literally begged their parents to divorce.

It is true that primary residence is often granted to the mothers. Some women tend to think this implies that the children belong 90 per cent to the mother and 10 per cent, or less, to the father. They regard the father's visitation to the child as a cumbersome irritation in their lives, as if the child is her puppy, and he is only allowed to play with her puppy when it suits her, or worse, when he pays her for the privilege. They will make it most unpleasant and sometimes virtually impossible for the father to visit the child. Some move to other towns, some just do not answer the phone when the father calls, some organise sports, family events or sleepovers on the father's weekends.

I agree that some fathers do the same. One father would arrange expensive luxury vacations abroad during the mother's allocated vacation and invite the children. The mother felt bad depriving her children of these opportunities and forfeited many of her vacations. She had to work, because she was one of those women who got the raw deal in the divorce settlement and often that would mean the children would just have to accompany her to work during their vacations.

She lost out with the divorce settlement and she lost out on her time with her children.

Children grow up and eventually they uncover the truth. Now they adore their independent, gorgeous, mature mother and soon enough they will treat her to vacations abroad.

When children are denied access to a parent this can constitute Parental Alienation Syndrome (PAS). I have testified in a court case where the mother attempted to alienate their son from his father. The judge ordered the lawyers to fetch the child from his mother's home and have him relocated to the father before 8pm that night and for the mother only to see the boy under supervision, henceforth.

Take note.

I have also testified in a case where a father battled for five years with very expensive court costs to regain access to his daughter, after the mother made a false allegation of sexual abuse. This is called SAID (sexual allegations in divorce syndrome). The little girl had thought her father had abandoned her, because restraining orders prevented her from having contact with him. The allegations were totally false, but it took five years to disprove.

Read more about: PARENTAL ALIENATION SYNDROME AND THE S.A.I.D. (SEXUAL ALLEGATIONS IN DIVORCE) SYNDROME on page 176 and 187

I am astounded that many divorcing couples have not been advised by their lawyers to read the Children's Act. For example, it is not just a parent who has a right of access to a child, it is the child who has a right of access to the parent, and to the extended family of that parent. It is not up to the mother to decide whom the child will see, where and for how long. The courts will decide this. Mothers who use children as weapons by sabotaging the father's access, do not realise in her petty attempt to spite the father, she is CONTRAVENING THE CHILDREN'S ACT.

Some mothers tend to reason if he is not paying maintenance or enough maintenance, she has the right to withhold him from seeing the child. Again, this is a contravention of the law. The child has a right to the father. She cannot sell that right. I agree it is a contravention for him not to pay maintenance, as well, but that issue is not linked to access. It is a separate issue, for which she can sue him, or attach an order to his salary. In both cases the child suffers.

The mother may be the holder of the primary residence, but she does not own 90 per cent of the child. If the child has sports activities on a weekend, the father can still fetch the child on the Friday night and take her to the hockey match on Saturday. There is no reason for him only to pick her up after the hockey match. There is no reason either for a father to return the child shortly after lunch on a Sunday because the child has to do homework for Monday. The father can supervise the homework over the weekend. If the father arrives 10 minutes late in collecting the child and the mother withholds the child "because the decree said 17h00", is she honestly acting in the best interest of her child, who has rights, or is she manifesting her bitterness, to the detriment of her child?

> **Case example:** One woman delighted in telling me how she punishes and humiliates her ex-husband before she allows him to see their son. He had finally divorced her after having had a long-standing affair, which she never knew about. I could understand her resentment and anger

towards the man, but demanding he send her an SMS explaining in graphic detail what a "low down, s**t, bast***, son of a b***, useless slug of a father he is," every time he wants to speak to or see their son, is spiteful, childish and unlawful. This is a typical example of a child being used as a weapon to punish another parent.

Case example: One man explained: "When I am married, my wife and children are family and I will protect them and woe to any enemy who tries to threaten them. When I divorce, my children remain my family. I will protect them and if the ex-wife tries to take them from me or prevents me from seeing them, she becomes the enemy."

Maintenance for children

Case example: One woman and her children moved in with husband no 2, who was quite affluent. Husband no 1 paid maintenance for the children, which she deposited in a separate bank account. Basically, husband no 2 covered the children's live-in expenses, without ever referring to the maintenance. One day when husband no 2 needed a cash amount for something, the wife offered him the accumulated maintenance. He was indignant. She could not understand why. I explained: "You should have offered him or paid the money over to him from the beginning to cover the children's costs. He was too much of a hero to ask you for it and silently provided for another man's children. He is a good provider. He will do this. Now you want to offer him your first husband's money, to help him out. Of course he will be offended. Firstly, because you kept the money, secondly because you are trying to help him financially which is an insult to him and thirdly the first husband is a nemesis to him." The husband explained if she had offered him the maintenance to cover the children's living expenses from the beginning, he would have appreciated the respect of the gesture, but he would have refused and suggested that she saved the money towards the children's further education or pay it to them when they reach 21. By not offering, she denied him the opportunity to be the magnanimous hero. Her offer came too late and too much silent resentment had accumulated, just like the interest on the money.

Some women are ignorant of the fact that both parents have a financial responsibility towards the children, and they become highly indignant when the court expects them to make a financial contribution. It is not just the father's baby, when it suits the mother, so to speak.

Some women are quite aware of the fact that they are also expected to pay maintenance for their children and therefore they fight nail and tooth to keep the children with them, so they can live off the maintenance the husbands are paying for the children and they can avoid paying for the children. These women are usually very reluctant to provide cash slips or receipts for the children's expenses, because they use the money for their own benefit. Many women buy toilet paper, household detergents, her expensive shampoo, perfume and make-up on the ex-husband's pharmacy account, which is supposed to be allocated to the children's medicinal requirements. "Because he can afford it, I am entitled to it," they justify their actions! One woman was quite willing to give her children up to the father, provided he claimed no maintenance from her and continued her monthly allowance.

Parenting Plans

Divorced parents need a Parenting Plan where such details as the education, religious matters, names, nicknames, maintenance, medical requirements, visitation rights etc. are agreed on by both parents. A registered mediator, lawyer, psychologist or other professional acknowledged by the Act can mediate this. For instance, parents can introduce a child to a religion, but it is against the Constitution that any religion be forced on any person. A Christian mother can take her son to church on her weekend and the Muslim father can take the son to Mosque on his weekend. Neither may prevent the other from exposing the child to a particular religion. The Parenting Plan can decree that children will not refer to stepmothers or stepfathers as Mom and Dad. The law stipulates that the Best Interest of the Child prevails, and that the Child's voice be heard. It is required that a person trained to work with children, such as a mediator, psychologist or social worker discuss this Parenting Plan with the child and if the child disagrees with it, the child can actually postpone the act of divorce. Of course the child's age and developmental phases are taken into consideration – leave that to the experts.

Parenting Plans can be registered with the Family Advocate's Office, that acts in the Best Interest of the Child. Ultimately the State is the upper custodian of all children in South Africa. Parents have rights and responsibilities. Unmarried fathers have rights and responsibilities too but they have to formally apply at the Children's Court, if they have not been living with the mother. Maintenance and their involvement in the child's life is taken into consideration. If a mother disputes paternity, then a DNA test can be done with a pathologist to determine paternity. All law firms can supply the Family Advocate's Office number and parents can contact the Institute for Mediators – who are not lawyers, but trained to mediate and registered by the State, as a less expensive option.

Ultimately it is in every person's best interest if divorces can be conducted in a mature, rational manner. I know this sounds impossible, but eventually people do recover from the emotional hurt and they move on and deep down, no matter their initial justifications or motivations, they will feel ashamed of their selfish, childish behaviour. Years down the line their adult children will want to know why the parents' spite was more important to them than their children's best interest at that time. When we have children, it implies that we become parents and parents put their children's best interest first. Grow up.

 Read more about: LIFE AS A SINGLE INDEPENDENT WOMAN on page 194

Why do ex-wives have such a hold on some men? The residue of the anti-hero

> Case example: I observed a man talking to his ex-wife over the phone. The ex-wife was demanding more maintenance for the children. He was getting very impatient with her. The current wife was listening to the conversation. She

tapped the husband on the shoulder. "Tell her she is being unreasonable. We just don't have the money," she said. Whereupon the husband promptly waved the wife away with his hand, gave her a dirty look and turned his back on her. The wife retreated to the bedroom and slammed the door. The man now had two women angry at him. So he went out for a beer, or two or three. The wife could not understand why he was nasty towards her. I explained: Talking to an ex-wife is stressful to a man because he has already been the anti-hero to that woman and men detest being the anti-hero; he wants to compensate for being the anti-hero, not because he wants to please the ex-wife, but because it makes him feel better about himself. Secondly, you were telling him what to do and say, which implies he is an idiot who can't communicate with his ex. Thirdly, you were implying that he does not earn enough, so he is a bad provider. That is a big insult. When the husband arrived home later that night, he was in a fighting mood. The wife looked at him and said: "Do you want to fight, or do you want to make love?" (She actually used the F-word). Later when they emerged from the bedroom he sheepishly remarked: "Now I remember why I married this one. She understands me."

Why do some men go out of their way to please their ex-wives? They seem to jump every time she snaps her fingers? This is a major bone of contention to second wives. The simple reason is because he disappointed that woman – he was the anti-hero. He will do anything to make up for it. He will perpetually try to please her, so he can feel better about himself. It is not about her, it's about him. Probably in their marriage she kept raising the bar and for years and years he was conditioned into believing his efforts were just never enough. So he tried harder and harder to make her smile. Eventually he called: "Enough!" and left her, but whenever they make contact, he regresses back into that "I have to try harder" mode. The man should realise that this woman is unhappy in herself. No matter what he does, he will never satisfy her. He will never be her hero. Let it go. Some dragons will never be slain. At home, in his castle, there may just be another new woman, who does actually appreciate him and he can be the most wonderful hero to her. When he dances for his ex-wife, he is being the anti-hero for the current wife too. Being the anti-hero to two women – the math just do not add up. Do the common sense pragmatic thing and be the hero to the current wife. You will get more sex.

Why do ex-wives make the men's lives hell? Because they get away with it.

Why do some men confess their financial failures to the ex-wife, but the current wife is the last one to find out? Because he has already been the anti-hero to the ex-wife and disappointed her. He cannot afford to be the anti-hero to the present wife, so he hides these circumstances from her. Will the ex-wife spitefully inform the current wife of their financial predicament? Chances are very good she will. Then he is in deeper trouble and he is the anti-hero to two women. Again. The math do not add up. Rather tell the current wife first. Women appreciate truthfulness. It makes them feel safe. IT MAKES THEM FEEL SAFE. Remember the part about the woman's intuition?

> **Case example:** I know of one second wife who discovered her husband had actually been to court to fight custody demands and took out another mortgage on the house, without telling her. The guilt of the deception drove him to drink. He just could not face his current wife. Finally he broke down. He realised heroes don't lie. His current wife forgave him, and they restructured their finances to pay off the outstanding maintenance. This woman had his back.

Mrs vs Mrs

I asked a man if it was fair for a second wife to want a new house and not move into the vacated space of the first Mrs. Women can tend to get emotional (illogical?) about this. He answered: "I can understand that she wants her own new house, but if I sell this place now, I lose too much on the bond. It is not a good time to sell."

Men are very aware of the financial knock they took during the divorce. Remember mostly it is the men who have to pay the women maintenance and not vice versa. Women usually forfeit the maintenance they receive from the first husband, when they marry the second. So divorced men are sensitive to women who make financial demands on them. "Why would she mind moving into another woman's space? If we move into a new house, she would also move into the previous owners' space, unless we build a brand-new house from scratch." "The thing is," I explained, "you did not make memories with another woman in that new house." "Can't we just repaint this one, then?" he asked. Yes, you can repaint it.

At least change the sheets and perhaps the bed.

> **Case example:** One woman told me the ex Mrs had the habit of wandering into the garden, cut the roses and took them home with her, because she (the first Mrs) had planted them. She did not want the second wife to have the pleasure of the roses!

> **Case example:** Many divorced men just keep the ex on the medical aid because it is convenient. However, when they remarry, we now have two Mrs' on the medical aid card. Dependent no 1 is the first Mrs, then Dependents numbers 2 and 3 and possibly 4 are the children and Dependent number 5 is the new Mrs. Nothing makes a woman feel as special as being number 5! It may sound illogical, but women are emotional and sensitive about these issues. If men expect women to take on their surnames, at least they can remove the ex Mrs from the medical aid, Christmas card list, mail box, answering machines, etc. Men usually forget to do this, or they think it is not practical to do it. Please remember where you are getting sex now.

One woman remarked to her husband who was reluctant to make the effort to remove his ex-wife from the lists: "Your loyalty should lie with the woman who has your back, the one behind whose back you lie at night. Not with the one who stabbed you in the back."

Exes stirring the pot

Many exes also have perverse fun in setting up their children as spies in the other household or generally just causing mischief. "You do not have to listen to her rules, she is not your mother." "Call me the moment your father's girlfriend arrives." Ex-wives often send their children to the new household with a list of do's and don'ts for the new wife to comply with. Some of them even colour code and laminate these rules! Alerting the other household of a child's allergies and medicinal requirements is fine. Prescribing what brand of vitamins the child should take, what washing powder is allowed and a specific brand of peanut butter is not. One father expected his new wife to wash, iron and fold the child's clothes and polish the shoes before he took the child home, just to keep the peace with the ex. Children can bring clothes and toys and take them home again, for it provides a sense of continuity to them, but I also advise that children should have their separate sets of clothes and toys at the alternate homes. It solves the complaints about dirty laundry, and it gives the child a sense of belonging and not feeling like an alien visitor in the second home.

> **Case example:** One stepmother awoke in the middle of the night to find her 10-year-old stepdaughter had cut a lock of her hair for her mother to use as muti. (Muti is traditional medicine, which may be used to cast a spell.) The father thought it was funny.

Some mothers call their children three or four or more times a day when the child is visiting the father. This prevents bonding, is intrusive and it sends the child the message that the child is not safe with the father. It also burdens the child with guilt complexes for leaving the mother or father alone at home. Calling once a day or once a weekend when they are older is quite sufficient. Children also often exploit situations and call the alternate parent as soon as the parent disciplines them or when they are not getting their way. It is amazing how parents compete to be the most popular parent, instead of just striving to be good parents.

Weekend dads and stepfathers

We have the brave hero out there on the battlefield and then out of no-where comes that fatal javelin that no-one could foresee. The blind spot inflicts a mortal wound. Freud coined the term: the Oedipus complex and his disciples developed the theory of the Electra complex, both based on Greek mythology.

At his birth it was prophesised that Oedipus, the young princeling of Thebes, would one day kill his father, the King. The King ordered the infant to be put to death, but he was secretly placed in foster care. As a young man he returned to Thebes, but on the way, he met and killed a man, not knowing it was his father the King. Oedipus became King of Thebes and unwittingly married the Queen widow, his mother. When he realised this he poked out his own eyes and travelled as a beggar. Freud used this Greek mythology to refer to the Oedipal developmental phase of 4 to 6 years, when boys subconsciously fall in love with the mother and compete with the father.

The flipside is called the Electra complex, when girls subconsciously fall in love with their fathers and compete with their mothers. The grand King of the Achaians, who waged the war against the Trojans, was called Agamemnon. He sacrificed his youngest daughter Iphigenia to secure favourable winds for the Greek fleet to cross the sea to Troy. Agamemnon's wife, Clytaemnestra never forgave him. Upon his triumphant return 10 years later to Mycenae, Clytaemnestra killed him. His remaining daughter Electra had waited patiently for her beloved father to return and when her mother killed her father, she mourned him and eventually plotted with her brother Orestes and killed her mother.

If I can single out one obstacle that causes major disputes and even break-ups of second marriages, then it would be THE CHILDREN. Both men and women have total blind spots concerning their children. This is a very difficult and sensitive, and contentious issue to discuss. However, there are solutions and it helps when parents can at least acknowledge that their children are their Achilles' heel.

Some fathers tend to be of the opinion that since they only see their children on weekends or holidays, the children are exempt from discipline or good manners during these times. The fathers do not want to spoil this short time with arguments or unpleasantness, so they "let bygones" slip by. The result is the stepmother having to cope with undisciplined, lazy, disrespectful children. To some fathers it is fine if the children lie on the couch all weekend watching television, or play on their tablets or cell phones, if they never clean up after themselves and these fathers expect their wives to cater, clean up and bite the bullet.

Fathers already feel like anti-heroes for abandoning their families and they are often blinded by a sense of guilt. They compensate by turning a blind eye and spoiling their own children rotten.

> **Case example:** A second wife was despondent with her husband's children just lying about all weekend, messing in the house, glued to their cell phones and generally getting on her nerves. I suggested that every child should get a chance to organise a family activity for Saturdays. This could be a picnic at the dam, visiting an expo, going fishing, visiting a food or flea market, a museum, volunteering at a welfare organisation, organising a treasure hunt, cleaning up a river, washing dogs at the SPCA, participating in a fun run, or attending a sports function, etc. It need not be an expensive excursion and they can take a packed lunch. The children can google activities or search newspapers for events. This gets them active and out of the house and there is family interaction. Saturday evenings they can watch television till 10pm and then retire to bed to allow the parents to watch television or better yet, the parents retire to their bedroom, undisturbed by 10pm. Sunday morning the kids and Dad make brunch. The wife can sleep late. (Because she prepared the Saturday lunches.) They all eat together; the kids clean up as much as they can and by 2pm it is time for the Dad to drive the kids home to their Mom who lives in another town. The wife then restores her home to normal and she has me-time. She can relax in a bubble bath for an hour. Dad comes home by 7pm and his wife is happy to see him and smiles as he enters the door. This arrangement worked perfectly. It provided time out of the house, family time, father and children bonding time and it gave her space on her own and with her husband. The children looked forward to the activities and weekends at Dad's became cool. After a few months, she realised she actually liked the children.

On the other hand, since the children are mostly allocated to the mother, the men often find themselves in the roles of stepfathers. Often subconsciously, or sometimes overtly, they miss their own children not living with them and resent their wives' children occupying that space. They resent paying for another man's children, especially if they are taken for granted. They also sometimes resent sharing her time and attention with the children. These same fathers may sometimes completely ignore the wife when his children arrive.

> **Case example:** A couple arrive home after a night out. Her son left the lights on and she makes a comment about him being inconsiderate again. "Yes," adds the husband, "and he left his plate in the lounge." "You never moan when your kids leave their dirty dishes all over the place," she snaps. This is a typical example of blind spotting. She is allowed to criticise her child, but the moment he does, all hell breaks loose and he has double standards regarding his children.

Parents have different discipline and rearing systems. It can be very confusing for children to switch from one system to another. In their mother's house they are allowed to take anything from the fridge at any time, at the Dad's house, they have to ask the stepmother's permission. At their mother's home they have to do chores to earn pocket money, at their Dad's home they have no chores, and he gives them money when they ask. In Mom's house both Mom and stepdad contribute to birthday presents, in Dad's house he buys gifts for his children and stepmom buys gifts for her children, which leads to one set of children having very expensive cell phones and the others have cheapies. The father feels it is his right to spoil his children, and the stepchildren's own father can buy them expensive cell phones. The children's own father feels he is already paying maintenance and they do not need expensive cell phones. The mother's heart is breaking because her children are feeling neglected. It is just not fair.

Even more confusing are different sets of rules for children in the same house. The wife's children, who live with the stepfather, have a curfew and chores during the week, but when his children come over for the weekend, they can watch television till late and they have no curfew or chores. Also, the stay-in children have to make space for the weekend children in their bedrooms, and the weekend children feel like alien invaders in their father's house, because they do not have their own beds and cupboard space. Complicated.

I have designed a discipline system that could work for all in both homes. It provides consistency and everybody knows what is expected of them. It works better if both homes implement the same system for all the children. Some parents absolutely refuse to co-operate with the other parent, insisting they know what is best for their children. If every parent knew what was best for their children all the time, why are there so many children in therapy?

 Read more about: DISCIPLINE PROTOCOL FOR CHILDREN on page 202

A new stepfather, who does not have children of his own, now suddenly has to cope with his new wife's children. Often these children overrule and dominate their mother, due to her guilt feelings, or she lacks the discipline that their father used to implement. Also, divorced mothers often indulge their children because the children become the source of love to her, that her ex-husband used to provide. The new stepfather feels it is his duty as man of the house to implement discipline and protect his wife. (After all, he fell in love with her, not her children.) More often than not, the mother puts her children first and secretly resents the new husband's interference and disciplining her children. She experiences it as personal criticism. A toxic atmosphere gradually permeates the home.

I would advise boyfriends who visit girlfriends with children, not to interfere in the children's discipline or lack there-of, especially if that boyfriend has no intention of permanently joining the domestic arrangement. It is a potential mine field he should rather avoid. If he interferes and disciplines the children, he is conveying an unspoken message to her that he is taking on the role of stepfather and that he has intentions of permanently joining the family. Decide if you are going to become the stepfather, or just remain the boyfriend, and explain this to the woman involved, so she does not develop expectancies, or resent your interference. Remember the children are her blind spot and she will interpret your discipline as personal criticism. Some women also expect their boyfriends to regularly treat her children to lunches, movies and gifts, and vacations etc and she may resent him if he does not take out his cheque book readily. Some women expect the boyfriends to bring the children a little gift every time he takes her out, to compensate for the fact that the children are going to be without their mother's company for a few hours. If he does spoil the children, to score brownie points with her, again she may interpret this as an intention to join the family. The best way to solve this uncomfortable situation is to COMMUNICATE. Tell her that you like buying the children gifts because you happen to like them as individuals and not because you intend becoming their stepfather. Or tell her you are dating her, not her children.

Many women state in no uncertain terms that if the man does not accept or entertain her children, then it is a no-go. "I'm a package deal," they declare on the first date. Hold your horses, lady, you are casting him in the role of a potential husband. In his mind, he is just dating you, spending time with you and getting to know you. Incorporating your children into his plans is a major responsibility he will only consider when he considers committing to you. Dating is not committing.

Women, more often than men, make the fatal mistake of discussing their love lives, romances and even their sex lives with their children. Many a Hero has had to red-face a smug teenager who knows the intimate details of his love-making skills (or lack thereof!)

Children can be overt or covert saboteurs of their fathers' new marriage

Often the problem not only lies with the parents having blind spots regarding their children, but also with the children blatantly exploiting the situation.

Children relate to their parents as grown-ups who are obliged to gratify the children's needs. Children do not consider their parents as autonomous adults who may have their own needs, including their own love lives. Especially young children are very selfish, even narcissistic and we cannot expect anything else from them. Children are also very materialistic. Children operate from the stance that they own their parents and that they have first right to their parents' attention. "He was my father first before he became her husband". This is not necessarily right or wrong, but the impact it has on second marriages must be taken into consideration and it needs to be managed. Parents need to establish clear boundaries. There is a mother-father parental unit, whose main function centres around the children, but there is also a husband-and-wife unit, which is a completely separate issue and not the concern of the children.

Young children

As children mature, they are supposed to develop an understanding of their parents being adults with their own needs, independent of the needs of the child, though adults do need to consider younger children's insecurities and developmental limitations and "be the better person". Children need to be disciplined and raised to become productive, law abiding citizens, who can function in complicated communities. How can we expect children to respect other people's rights, if we do not respect their rights?

> **Case example:** A father gave his nine-year-old daughter a gorgeous doll for her birthday. The family moved to a new home and when the little girl came over for the weekend visit, she asked her stepsister where her stepmother had packed the dolls, for she could not find her gorgeous doll. "My mother gave all our dolls to her poor relatives. She said we were getting too old to play with dolls and those girls' parents could not afford dolls," the stepsister answered. The nine-year-old girl grew into an adult woman, but whenever she thought about that doll her heart broke and she still experienced the pain of a nine-year-old girl who was denied the right of ownership, just because she was a minor. She could not complain to her father about the loss of her doll, for she would sound unsympathetic towards the poor little girls, but the fact that an adult thought she had the right to dispose of that little girl's prized possession, without even discussing it with the girl, left a deep scar.

Young stepsiblings very often fight and argue, much the same as neighbours' children may do. Golden advice to parents would be not to get involved in every fight, not to take sides and let the children sort it out themselves. It teaches them conflict resolution. Unless of course one child is seriously being bullied by another one. House rules should apply to all children and double standards will only be exploited by all children.

Teenagers

By the time children become teenagers or young adults, it is not unreasonable for the new spouse to expect some form of respect and consideration from the stepchildren. However difficult this may be, parents need to overcome their blind spots and address this issue in a mature way.

> **Case example:** A second wife moved into her new husband's home. "Please make yourself at home," he invited. "It is your home now, so change anything you want and make it comfortable." The first thing she changed was the lay-out of the kitchen. She moved the crockery into different cupboards, replaced the worn-out blinds with bright yellow curtains and bought new dish cloths. She was very happy with her new kitchen. Until the first weekend his teenage daughters came over. The girls packed all the crockery back into their original places. "It is the way our Mom used to have it," they said. When the wife brought this under the attention of her husband, his response was: "It is only crockery, what does it matter where we keep it?" His answer illustrated a typical male pragmatic response. He also did not want to get involved in a catfight. What he did not realise was the subtle underlying nuance of his daughters sending his new wife the message: "You will never be the Queen of this house. We will not allow you. Our father will always take our side against you. You will always be the outsider." Men then wonder why they end up outside the wife's bed?

The above scenario can also happen in a home where daughters turn on the biological mother, because an Electra complex situation exists.

Many second wives are side-lined and actually excluded in such a manner. They are subtly reduced to second hand occupants in what is supposed to be their own new homes. They are barely tolerated and treated by the children with disdain as the woman their father sleeps with, not as the woman of the house.

Quite often men are also treated as an intruder and not as the head of the household, or even an equal adult decision maker and recognised disciplinarian. When parents condone this attitude in their children, to reduce the new partner to a subservient role and where it is acceptable for the kids to rule, then those parents should perhaps postpone getting married until the children have left home. Parents should gratify their children's needs to the best of their abilities and give them lots and lots of attention and affection. That is wonderful and loving, but to allow the children to rule the roost and oust the new spouse is actually detrimental to those children.

These children grow up thinking everybody should dance to their tunes, and they develop major adjustment problems later in their own relationships and at places of employment, when their partners and colleagues do not consider it so cute.

> **Case example:** Two teenage daughters wandered into the stepmother's bathroom and promptly used her expensive make-up without her permission. When she complained, the father took them to the shops and bought them their own expensive make-up. He thought he was solving the problem pragmatically. What he did not realise, is he was rewarding his children for using someone else's property without permission. He could have bought them the make-up after they had apologised.

It is not only the stepmother who is side-lined, but also the stepfather, who often experiences a total lack of respect.

Heroes need to be appreciated and respected for being the providers, especially when they are providing for other men's children.

> **Case example:** One man complained when he arrives home every day after a long day's labour, he always has to

get out of his car and remove his stepson's bicycle from the driveway, to gain access to the garage. When he walks into the home his wife is cooking – she does not even turn to greet him properly. He cannot sit in the lounge and watch the news or enjoy a drink because his stepdaughter is lying on the couch watching soaps and his stepson is in his study, playing games on his computer. Neither of the children greet him properly either. He came home one day and drove over the bicycle with his 4x4, unplugged the television and kept his study door locked. His wife complained he was being unreasonable.

One father expected his new wife to fetch his teenage boy from a private school hostel every Friday afternoon. She did this without complaint and took him shopping to fill the house with snacks that he liked to eat during the weekend. The boy complained bitterly when the couple went out over the weekend since he demanded his father's attention and claimed they could go out during the week when he was in the hostel. He had no consideration for the fact that his father worked during the week, that he may be exhausted earning a living to pay for the boy's tuition fees and that he would also just like to relax over the weekend with his wife. The father complied with the son's wishes to avoid a tantrum. Men detest it when women tell them what to do, but often they allow their children to rule the roost.

Young adults

One would expect young adult children to have developed insight into their parents' adaptation to second marriages and to exhibit less self-centred immature behaviour.

> Case example: A man's 18-year-old daughter comes to visit for a vacation. Every evening she sits next to her Dad on the couch, watching television, while the second wife cooks. They all eat on trays in front of the television. Everyone takes their own tray back to the kitchen. Whilst the wife unpacks the trays, the young lady rushes back to the lounge and plonks herself next to her father again, swinging her legs over his lap. He naturally puts his arm

around his daughter. After cleaning up the kitchen the wife enters the lounge. She would now like to relax and have time with her husband, whom she has not seen all day. There is another woman in her place next to her husband. Must she now sit on one of the chairs? If she retreats to the bedroom to read a book, she is accused of being unsociable. If she complains that the daughter is not helping with dinner or cleaning up afterwards, his defense is that the daughter is on vacation. If the wife complains that the daughter is sitting on her place, the husband accuses her of being jealous of his child. So his wife, who is supposed to be his metaphorical queen, is expected to serve the little princess. The little princess is usurping the queen's throne. Does he really wonder why he is not getting sex? It is fine for the daughter to cuddle next to her Dad, but as soon as the wife enters, either the daughter should move of her own accord, or the father can shoo her off gently to make space for his wife. In case this sounds unfair, how would the father feel if his wife's teenage son is forever sitting on her lap? How would he feel if the only time he gets to be with his wife is when she gets into bed at night, and then she is tired?

Case example: One man had two grown daughters. Wherever he went, each daughter would grab a hand and the second wife would have to trail behind them. Even when they travelled abroad, the daughters would sit next to the father on the plane. When they had dinner in a restaurant, the daughters sat on each side of him. When the father held his wife's hand in public, the daughters would walk right up to him, throw their arms around his neck and kiss him on the mouth. His wife grew grumpy when the daughters argued who should sit in the front seat of the car next to the Dad. I kid you not! This woman had virtually no private space of her own, not even in her bedroom and she had no personal access to her husband. She could not wait for him, dressed in sexy lingerie in bed at night, for the girls would lie on the parents' bed

145

watching television, waiting for the father to get home. The husband seemed oblivious that his wife was being ousted and alienated by his daughters. He thought she was just jealous. What is the purpose of being married to a man if a wife has to queue to cuddle him and to compete for a scrap of recognition and attention?

One would think this situation would improve when these daughters got married. At least they were out of the home, but the moment they visited, they abandoned their husbands and still sat on their father's lap. It is cute when a five-year-old sits on her father's lap.

It is not so cute when she is 25. Eventually this man saw the light and set the boundaries. Else he would have grown old a very lonely man.

Not only the girls, but also the boys make it very difficult for their parents to get on with their lives.

Case example: Another young prince was a third-year student. He did not want to live in a dormitory nor did he want to move into a commune, because he did not want to share a bathroom with other students. So he stayed with his father and stepmother. He paid no rent, had a television and wi-fi in his room, the housekeeper attended to his laundry and ironed his clothes. He had a brand-new car and his Dad paid for a tank of petrol every so often. He was still a dependent on his Dad's medical aid and his Dad paid for his studies, and books. He also paid him an allowance each month and the prince supplemented this by acting as a mentor to first year students. He spent his money socialising with his friends. He often criticised his stepmother's housekeeping skills and one day they had a big blow-up due to the fact that his stepmother refused him permission to invite six friends to sleep over one night when they all had too much to drink. "There are enough spare bedrooms in my father's house," he complained. What he did not consider was that the housekeeper would have to wash six sets of bed linen the next day, fit them all in on the washing line and iron 12 sheets and 12 pillow cases as well as six duvet covers. The stepmother felt this

146

was too much work to disrupt her household just to indulge the prince and his drunken entourage. The prince called her wicked.

Case example: Another student princess was only prepared to move out if her father provided her with a fully furnished flat, close to the university. She had already hand-picked the leather couches, washing machine and tumble dryer. Heaven forbid to suggest a laundrette, and she refused to return home every weekend with her dirty laundry for her stepmother to wash, for that would defy the purpose of living on her own, independently! I wondered if she had ever washed a sheet in her life or sewed on a button? Imagine the lucky young man who just can't wait to marry her? Or the lazy bum, who happens to be in-between jobs and who cannot be a waiter because it interferes with his artistic creativity, who moves in with her for free?

Sometimes parents have problems coming to terms with their children growing up.

A particularly explosive situation is when teenage stepsiblings fall in love with another. What happens when her 17-year-old son falls in love with his 15-year-old daughter and they all sleep under one roof over weekends? Many parents are often oblivious to this quite common occurrence.

Parents are entitled to their values and every person has the right to set rules in their own homes, but children over the age of legal consent need no-one's permission to have sex. Once they turn 21, one can ask them to respect rules out of consideration, but they are adults and one can no longer prevent them. New rules, new boundaries and reciprocal respect are terms to be renegotiated when adult children live with their parents.

Case example: A 25-year-old young man enjoyed the privilege of still living in the same house as his parents. His girlfriend often slept over. His mother complained to me she could not understand why the 'children' kept their bedroom door locked. In the morning she wanted to open the door to let the dog out, but it would be locked. "They are probably having sex," I remarked. Her jaw dropped and her eyes grew large. She was stunned. She never considered that her son was a man, who actually had sex.

Adult children failing to launch often place severe stress on their parents' finances.

Developmental phases continue far beyond teenage years. Parents in their 50s are concerned about their retirement funds and basically deserve the peace of mind that they can reap the rewards of 30 to 40 years of hard work. Young adult children failing year after year of university or young adults who do not search for and find employment are exploiting their parents' goodwill and blind spots. Grow up. Get a job.

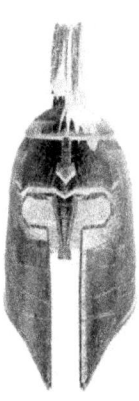

THE SEASONED HERO – SECOND TIME AROUND

The recovered divorced man has several new partnership options, more than the recovered divorced woman. He can date younger never-been-married-before women, divorced women with or without children, or widows. Divorced women can usually only date divorced men or widowers. Some women find younger-never-been-married men, but mostly they do not. Toy boys are expensive.

Who are his options?

Some divorced parents are seriously only looking for a partner to help them raise their children. Custody of children are often granted to mothers. Many young divorcees in their 30s struggling to get by on insufficient maintenance, or single mothers, are desperately trying to catch a wealthy divorced man, to pay for their children's tuition and secure their future. The easiest way to catch such a man of course is by falling pregnant. It is quite shocking how many women still catch a man by falling pregnant and how many men still fall for this. When I warn the men of this possibility, they give me that double-take look, which means they never considered that it could happen to them.

Some women in their 40s and 50s find themselves in a predicament where their husbands left them for younger women, or just walked out because they had had enough. Some of these women walked out because they had had enough. Whatever the reason, they suddenly find themselves in a situation where they have a tremendous loss of income, or no income, for husbands are not obliged to pay maintenance forever. These women have no property in their names, no pension provision, no annuities and they suddenly have to work, while they have been out of the market for years. They have no skills and no experience. They endure a serious downgrade in their lifestyle, and they resent this. They feel that life has cheated them. They got a raw deal. They are angry at themselves for giving up doing their own thing when they got married or never having cultivated their own thing in the first place. The fantasy or expectancy of "catching a rich husband and becoming a not-having-to-work-stay-at-home-Mom" bombed out. Their resentment is quite clear in their attitude and relations towards men, yet they hope to land themselves a rich man to regain and maintain their previous lifestyle. They have to compete with younger divorcees but at least the older women's children have left the nest.

The men are once bitten twice shy and they run rings around these women. They do not want to be caught in bitter divorce settlements with women who are after their money, for a second time. They are already supporting their ex-wives and paying maintenance for their children. They do not want the financial burden of looking after another man's children. So they date the women, but shy away from commitment. These women now find themselves in the very difficult position where they have to find employment and make provision for retirement. Some women are desperate enough to fall pregnant deliberately, especially if they have no income. Some men may not regard themselves as affluent men or a catch, so they do not take precautions, but to a desperate woman, who feels unsafe, any income he may earn is rich to her. If she cannot stand on her own two feet after a divorce, and start earning her own living, what makes him think she will support him and have his back, when things may go bad for him?

This is a bleak picture. Does love not enter the equation anywhere? The upside is if there was no hope, why would there be so many people on dating sites seriously looking for partners? (Granted, some are just looking for sex.) People still want to be together and despite the odds, they are still hoping for love. Heroes do get second or even third chances of being someone else's hero. Some people learn from their mistakes, some do not. Some heroes still confuse "rescuing" with a heroic act. It is not.

Some seasoned older divorced heroes honestly believe they can date or marry very young women in their 20s. As I told one of my middle-aged male friends: "Show me the queue of young nymphomaniacs lining up outside? Let's face it, you are no longer the pick of the litter either, and unless you have a six-digit bank balance and looking for a real bimbo, rather settle for the woman who has also been around the block and who can appreciate you for the hero you are, warts and all." He did and he is happily married today.

Baldies and Bimbo's

When a man feels his libido slipping away, he may enter what is commonly called the "midlife crisis." Besides buying himself the most expensive toys he can afford – or can't afford – a compulsory item is the young nymph at his side.

When we investigate the relationship between a man in his late 50s and a young woman in her mid-20s, we may find benefits for both. The woman may be suffering from a narcissistic disorder. In this relationship she will be complimented on her beauty daily by her man. He will shower her with gifts and parade her in glittering finery. He will pay for cosmetic surgery and treat her to vacations in Mauritius to acquire a tan, and to St Moritz to show it off. She will get all the attention Cinderella and all the other fairytale princesses ever hoped for. She will be the main attraction of the show.

He gets sex. And sex and sex. And perhaps the envy of a few other misguided heroes out there.

151

They would only socialise with his friends – he has the power and the money, so he calls the shots. Initially she will not mind, for she has no competition among the elderly matrons married to his friends. Imagine the dinner conversation when one of these wives turns to our Princess and says: "So how was school today, Dearest?" For what other topic would these mature women discuss with one who might be younger than their daughters?

Soon enough our precious Princess would no longer find it fun to socialise with his friends. She may pout and complain that they should be having fun with her friends. There is no hope in hell little Princess, that he would compete with the young Adonis' of your peer group. He knows he would be the joke of the town, if he moves in her circles.

Now would this couple have children? She may fall pregnant, just to secure his undying devotion, but falling pregnant will affect her perfect physique and highlight that she may be getting older and then he may trade her in for the next 23-year-old. Grandpas get very grumpy when screaming babies and smelly diapers spoil their access to Venus.

Does she enjoy the sex? Do not fool yourself Jolly Roger regarding your perceived virility. Why would she prefer to have sex with a crinkle-skinned, potbellied, balding, tooth decayed or dentured, trembling old Nestor on Viagra, when she can have virile Achilles? The Princess is there because she feels safe – as long as her beauty outlasts him. If it does and he dies, he exits a happy man who had lots of sex right up to the end, and she gets the money. As I said, it can be a mutually beneficial arrangement.

What is rather ridiculous is that the greying old man chasing the young girl who calls him uncle, honestly believes that she may be interested in him, as a virile man. Old men who believe having sex with a girl half his age will revitalise his libido, are as ridiculous and stupid as the myth that sleeping with a virgin will cure Aids. Most young women call them sleazy, slimy, dirty, yucky, goofy, nasty and smelly, like seven randy little dwarfs lusting after Snow White.

On the contrary, older men who may have a twinkle in the eye, but who behave with dignity, are charming and all women like talking to them because they find them distinguished, interesting, wise and they feel safe. Generally, girls flock around the men whom they feel safe with.

Another complication of older men dating girls young enough to be their daughters is that mature women observe this behaviour and shy away from these immature men. It is not because the more mature women feels she cannot compete with the physical attractiveness of the younger female, it is rather because she is not inclined to waste her time with a male who is still fixated on physical youthful beauty and who has not yet discovered the richness of experience, maturity, sharing, friendship, comfortable camaraderie, humor and health in a relationship.

The seasoned Hero may be lucky and wise enough to attract a mature free spirit.

Mature free spirits

Men often complain that all women just want to get married. This is simply not true. (It is as false as the statement that all men want sex all the time.) There are independent women – with adult children or without children – who are free spirits. Does it ever occur to men that there may be women out there who are not that eager to tie the knot either? Not because they resent or hate all men, but because they enjoy doing their own thing. They have established themselves in their own independent lives, with their own homes, friends, interests, financial status, etc. Independent does not mean bossy. Because she values her independence, she can also respect his. Because she worked hard to earn her money, she understands the importance of his quest. These women would appreciate a life partner, lover, friend with benefits, travelling companion. They do not require the proverbial picket fence and would much rather pack their bags and go off on an adventure. They may not view every relationship as necessarily aiming for the church aisle, but they do require maturity, which would solidify a relationship. They do not need marriage, but they do want solid relationships. They are too mature for games. Loyalty, fidelity, honesty, tolerance, friendship, integrity, humor and extended gratification of needs are qualities of maturity. These women like sex. I repeat: they like and enjoy sex, and by now, they are good at it, but they do not just sleep with men indiscriminately. They sleep with men whom they have feelings for and who have feelings for them. And if men are not mature enough to deal with those emotions, then they should move on and lose out. As I noted before, if a man cannot man-up to his emotions, then he cannot man-up to a mature woman's bed. A person's psyche is a circle comprised of three segments: the physical, emotional and cognitive. To deny one or fragment one, would imply that the circle is incomplete. To integrate all three, indicates maturity, a wholeness. There may be battle scars, but despite the previous hurt or injuries, the person has managed to deal with them, and does not define him or herself as a victim. Mature women, who have integrated their sexuality, date mature men who have integrated their emotions. When a man owns-up and acknowledges his feelings, it is a sign of strength and maturity, not a weakness.

Having feelings does not by default imply that these women want to get married, but if they happen to get married, it is for totally different reasons than when they donned the wedding dress in their youth. To these women, marriage may mean a union of two independent mature people, who enter a contract willingly. It can be a voluntary consenting attachment, not a compulsory dependency. It is not about expectations, it is about sharing. Sharing time, sharing space, sharing confidences and vulnerabilities, sharing a bed, sharing adventures, sharing humor, with the added benefit that only experience can bring. The sex can be exciting and invigorating, because it is shared and appreciated.

Blessed are the couples who weathered the storms and endured and who no longer seek the young love of Apollo's dolphins playing in the frothy waves, but rather know a deeper love like the undercurrent of

154

Poseidon's ocean – a love with the power of a tsunami. The love of the seasoned Hero and the ageless Goddess. How is that? Sounds right to me.

Fare thee well, Odysseus.

INTROVERTS AND EXTRAVERTS

The psychologist Carl Jung coined the terms Introvert and Extravert.

When I ask people, what is the difference between extraverts and introverts, they respond that introverts do not like socializing. This is not the case. The difference is when there is a stimulus - something happens - the extravert immediately reacts outwards, while the introvert internalizes the information, processes it and then responds to it. It is in the response to the stimuli where the difference lies, not in their social interaction per se.

Since they incorporate information - taking it in - introverts need time alone to process the information. This is why introverts need "space". They like being on their own, thinking about things. When introverts withdraw, extraverts experience this as rejection. It is not rejection, it is merely processing time. Imagine a computer needs to process information. If we keep tapping the keyboard, it will either freeze or explode. Do not tap the keyboard of the introvert when they need space. Leave them alone until they are ready to interact.

Extraverts want attention 24/7. They cannot stand being alone. They cannot understand that the introvert voluntarily wants to be alone. Extraverts are always looking for company and stimuli and if they do not find it, they create it. Introverts avoid it.

Introverts are like cats. When they encounter a stranger for the first time, they ignore him. They may walk past a few times without acknowledging the stranger. They are not rude, haughty, shy or dumb. They are introverts. Do not pick up the cat. The cat is getting accustomed to your energy. If it likes you, it will make eye contact. Now you can stroke it gently. Do not pick up the cat. One day the cat will jump on your lap and purr and be all over you. Now you can pick up the cat and play with it. It may even sleep with you. Introverts know it is rude not to at least greet strangers, but they would rather not. Not until they have sussed them out.

Extraverts are like dogs on a beach. They sniff each other's backsides, wag their tails and off they go, friends for life. They are spontaneous.

Introverts are reserved. Extraverts are busy, they talk and laugh and vibrate. Introverts contemplate, develop insight and cruise.

One introvert man said he could remember being so irritated by his first wife who always wanted to know what he thought about a movie the moment they left the cinema. If they understand each other, introverts and extraverts will realise neither is right or wrong, they are just different.

Introverts do not like noise. Since they are processing information all the time, it is very noisy inside their heads. That is why they abhor additional noise. They cannot listen to you, the radio and the tv at the same time. They do not like crowds or noisy places. Too much stimuli. Extraverts love noise. When they walk into a home, they switch on the tv, the radio and they sing. Introverts run for the hills. Because introverts are usually very quiet at first, extraverts often ask them what is wrong. Nothing is wrong, they are thinking, that is all.

Extraverts think when people are not talking, they are unhappy. So they keep asking the introvert:

"What is wrong?"

"Nothing."

"What is wrong?"

"NOTHING!"

"See I knew something is wrong."

Stop jabbing the keyboard. Some introverts are shy, some are not. They just do not have something meaningful to say at that point in time and they do not like small talk. Extraverts can chatter away all day long.

When introverts enter a restaurant, they aim for the corners with their backs to the walls, where they can observe the people, but stay out of sight. Extraverts aim for the middle of the restaurant and within five minutes they have made friends with the waiter, the patrons at the next table and the chef. Introverts just want to eat in peace. Do not put an introvert on the spot by introducing them to everybody at once and expect them to please everybody. Give them time. Please.

If you invite an introvert to a function over the weekend, their first answer is "No". Give them time to think about it and probably by Friday they will say yes and go, and have a good time. Up to a point. Once introverts have blended people's energy, they can be very funny, witty and very sociable. They can be the life of a party, if they want to and if they feel comfortable with the people. However, too much stimuli tires them, so by 12 pm they want to go home. By 12 pm, however the extraverts' batteries are fully charged and they want to stay longer, and longer and longer. Best go with two cars.

Extraverts can be warm and sociable, funny and bubbly. They move towards people when they feel insecure and they need affirmation. They act out. Introverts can also be warm, funny and sociable but they withdraw when they feel insecure. They can wallow in self-pity.

Extraverts can be gregarious, bigger than life, and they always seem to have so much fun. Some introverts feel intimidated by extraverts and they may feel there is something wrong with them because they are not like the extraverts. There is nothing wrong being an introvert. Half of the population are introverts. They just do not make so much noise as the extraverts and that is why you do not notice them. Look to the quiet corners - they are there, one-on-one solving the world's serious problems. Or laughing quietly at the spectacles of the extraverts. Introverts have much fun too - mostly inside their heads.

Open plan offices do not work with introverts. Please allow them their cubicles or at least position them along the walls with high enough partitions to provide them privacy - if you want them to be productive. Position the extraverts in the middle, facing each other, where they thrive on open competition. If you position introverts in noisy open plan offices, they will resign or become disgruntled.

In a marriage I advise the extravert to turn the volume down a little and expect less, and the introvert to up the volume and give a little more. Allow the introvert the long lonely bike ride on a Saturday morning - the me-time - and they will accompany the extravert to the noisy dinner party that night.

Introverts should be aware of the impact they have on others. Once the extravert knows how to extend the introvert time to process, the introvert sometimes forgets to give feedback. So by Friday the poor extravert still does not know if he is going to that party that he enquired about three days ago.

Friends may visit the introvert-extravert couple. Soon enough the introvert will excuse him/herself and pull a disappearing act. They either go to sleep or find something else to do, away from the people. They may wash the dishes in the kitchen, just to be able to take a mini me-time break. Understand this and accommodate it.

Another tip for the introvert is to smile more. At a function or social event if you smile, then the extraverts think you are happy and approve of them, so they will not ask you what is wrong. Smile and continue your own private thoughts and just nod your head now and again. People may just benefit from your sharing those private thoughts - that is if the extravert gives you a chance to talk.

My father compared introverts and extraverts to bombers and fighter pilots during the Second World War. The bombers fly in formation and cause devastation by their clusters of bombs dropped indiscriminately. The fighter pilots fly alone, often coming directly out of the sun, when the enemy cannot see them, and they are precise, deadly snipers. In the canteen, the bombers sit together in the middle of the room, the fighter pilots sit alone at the bar.

Both extraverts and introverts can work with people. Extraverts are people-people. Introverts are one-on-one people. Both may have empathy, but extraverts spontaneously express their feelings. Introverts may feel deeply, but they do not share those feelings easily. Extraverts may be warm, but superficial. Introverts may seem cynical, but actually they feel too much.

Cats and dogs can live in harmony together as long as they respect their differences.

TIME OUT

Time-Out is a life skill tool that any one of the parties can call during a heated argument and the other person has to adhere, for the sake of the relationship, personal dignity and self-respect.

The procedure of Time-Out work as follows:

We call Time-Out when we reach that point in the argument where we are about to lose control, either by saying things we should not, or worse, where we may just resort to violence.

If any person calls Time-Out, then the parties retreat, each to a different safe haven. This can be to the bedroom, the garden outside, bathroom etc. Just get away from each other.

Now you can continue the argument on a virtual platform with the partner, venting all your anger and releasing all the dirty name calling burning inside your guts, in a room or space where no-one but yourself can hear it. At first, we focus on the other person: "You are a lousy, low down snake." "You are a manipulating bitch." Carry on until you have nothing left to say. The aim of this part of the exercise is just to vent and rid yourself of the anger – which is a destructive emotion.

Then we shift gears and we express our feelings: "I am angry, I am hurting, I feel betrayed, I am disappointed, I feel lost, I feel trapped..." Cry if needs be. Bury your face in the pillow. Just let it out. The aim of this part of the exercise is to get in touch with your feelings and express them. Tell yourself what you are feeling. This helps you to ground yourself and to get a hold of yourself.

When all is out of your system, now investigate your own point of view re the argument. Are you really 100%, right? Are there matters where you can concede or compromise? Remember no-one can hear you and argue with you at this point. Just consider that you may not be 100% right.

Now re-evaluate the partner's point of view. Even if it does not make sense, see if you can at least repeat their point of view, just to make sure that you actually heard it. But do make an effort to find some truth or justification or make sense from it. You do not have to agree with it, just try to figure it out and consider it.

Ask yourself if the issue that you are arguing about is going to be important in six months' time?

Is there perhaps a hidden subtext underlying this issue, that is more important and that you are both ignoring.

If the issue will not be important in six months' time, go out and make up, even if you were right and the other party was wrong. Your marriage is more important than being right.

If there is a subtext, at least acknowledge that there may be a bigger problem which may require professional help and in the meantime, call a truce.

Go out and find a more friendly and amicable way to call a truce. Is it really worth a few days' sulking?

Apologies can always help. Even if you are not apologising for your behaviour or whatever the perception is that you did wrong, at least be sorry that you hurt the other person's feelings. This is after all the person that you love and that you want to be with.

Time-Out should not exceed an hour. If you cannot calm down within an hour at least go out and tell the partner that you are still upset and that you would prefer to talk about it the following day. Then go to bed and sleep.

Time-Out can only be called when both parties have at least had a chance to say something. A person cannot say: "I am angry because you came home late" and before the other person can even explain or defend, you call Time-Out. Time-Out is not a tool to silence the other person. It is a tool to control your own anger.

Self-control and self-discipline are easy words to use when we are calm. It is in the heat of the moment when it requires almost super human effort to apply it. This is what makes us mature adults. We take responsibility to vent our anger without destruction.

MASLOW'S THEORY ON THE HIERARCHY OF NEEDS

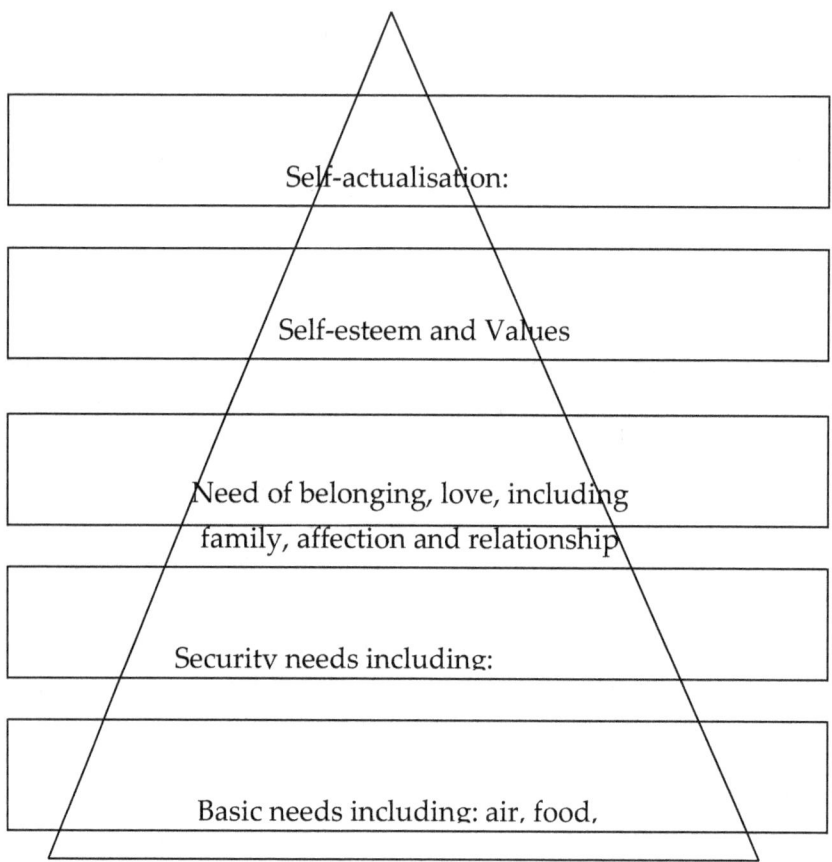

Self-actualisation:

Self-esteem and Values

Need of belonging, love, including family, affection and relationship

Security needs including:

Basic needs including: air, food,

In his book, Motivation and Personality (1970 2nd edition Harper & Row) psychologist Maslow postulated that human behavior is motivated by a hierarchy of basic needs. Once lower needs are gratified, the organism – or human – will escalate to higher needs. A basic need will dominate behavior if it is thwarted or when the organism is deprived of it. Once the need is gratified, it releases its domination of the organism.

Physiological needs comprise the bottom tier of the hierarchy. These are our basic human needs, such as hunger, thirst, sleep, sex and warmth. If a need has been continuously satisfied in the past, we are better equipped to deal with its deprivation in future. If not, we may always subconsciously yearn for the gratification of that unfulfilled basic need.

The second tier of needs encompass those for safety, including such concepts such as security, stability, dependency, protection and freedom from fear as well as from anxiety and chaos, need for structure, order, law, limits, strength in the protector, etc. Maslow explains should these needs not be fulfilled "the organism may equally well be wholly dominated by them... and we may then fairly describe the whole organism as a safety-seeking mechanism."

Maslow identified the third tier as the need for belongingness and love. Losing touch with our roots, relocating often and changing schools, forced resettlement, war, etc. will all impact on our sense of belonging. If we never experience receiving love, how can we be expected to give it?

The fourth tier comprises "esteem" needs. According to Maslow these are the desire for strength, achievement, adequacy, mastery and competence, confidence, status, glory dominance, recognition, dignity and appreciation. To men, money represents status and recognition in the eyes of other men.

The fifth and last tier, is the need for self-actualization. To Maslow, this represents a human being's need to achieve his / her highest altruistic potential.

CHARACTERISTICS OF SELF-ACTUALIZED PEOPLE

MORE EFFICIENT PERCEPTION OF REALITY AND MORE COMFORTABLE RELATIONS WITH IT:

They have an unusual ability to detect the spurious, the fake and the dishonest in a personality and in general to judge people correctly and efficiently. They do not cling to the familiar, nor is their quest for the truth a catastrophic need for certainty, safety, definiteness, and order. They can be, when the total objective situation calls for it, comfortably disorderly, sloppy, anarchic, chaotic, vague, doubtful, uncertain, indefinite, approximate, inexact or inaccurate.

ACCEPTANCE (SELF, OTHERS, NATURE)

They tend to be good to animals, hearty in their appetites and enjoying themselves without regret or shame or apology. Closely related to their self-acceptance and to acceptance of others is 1) their lack of defensiveness, protective coloration, or pose and 2) their distaste for such artificialities in others. Cant, guile, hypocrisy, front, face, playing a game, trying to impress in conventional ways: these all are absent in themselves to an unusual degree.

SPONTANEITY, SIMPLICITY AND NATURALNESS

Their unconventionality is not superficial but essential and internal. It is their impulses, thought, consciousness that are so unusually unconventional, spontaneous and natural. Apparently recognizing that the world of people in which they live could not understand or accept this, and since they have no wish to hurt them or fight with them over every triviality, they will go through the ceremonies and rituals of convention with a good-humored shrug and with the best possible grace. When they consider something very important, it will be at such moments that their essential lack of conventionality appears, and not with the average Bohemian or authority-rebel, who makes great issues of trivial things and who will fight some unimportant regulation as if it were a world issue.

One consequence of this characteristic is that they have codes of ethics that are relatively autonomous and individual rather than conventional.

The unthinking observer might sometimes believe them to be unethical, since they break down not only conventions but laws when the situation seems to demand it. Sometimes they let themselves go deliberately, out of momentary irritation with customary rigidity or with conventional blindness. They may for instance, be trying to teach someone or they may be trying to protect someone from hurt or injustice or they may sometimes find emotions bubbling up from within them that are so pleasant or even ecstatic that it seems sacrilegious to suppress them.

Their ease of penetration to reality, their closer approach to an animal-like or childlike acceptance and spontaneity imply a superior awareness of their own impulses, desires, opinions and subjective reactions in general.

PROBLEM CENTERING

They are problem centered rather than ego centered. They generally are not problems for themselves and are generally not much concerned about themselves. Eg as contrasted with the ordinary introspectiveness that one finds in insecure people. These individuals customarily have missions in life, some task to fulfill, some problem outside themselves which enlists much of their energies.

They work within a framework of values that are broad and not petty, universal and not local, and in terms of a century rather than the moment. In a word, these people are all in one sense or another philosophers, however homely.

THE QUALITY OF DETACHMENT: THE NEED FOR PRIVACY

All of them can be solitary without harm to themselves and without discomfort. Furthermore, it is true for almost all that they positively like solitude and privacy to a definitely greater degree than the average person.

They have an ability to concentrate to a degree not usual for ordinary men or women. Intense concentration produces as a by-product such phenomena as absent-mindedness, the ability to forget and to be oblivious of outer surroundings.

Another meaning of autonomy is self-decision, self-government, being an active, responsible, self-disciplined, deciding agent rather than a pawn or helplessly determined by others.

AUTONOMY: INDEPENDENCE OF CULTURE AND ENVIRONMENT: WILL ACTIVE AGENTS

They are self-contained. They have become strong enough to be independent of the good opinion of other people or even their affection.

CONTINUED FRESHNESS OF APPRECIATION

They have a wonderful capacity to appreciate again and again freshly and naively the basic goods of life, with awe, pleasure, wonder and even ecstasy, however stale these experiences may have become to others. They derive ecstasy, inspiration, and strength from the basic experiences of life and none of them will get this same sort of reaction from going to a night club or getting a lot of money or having a good time at a party.

THE MYSTIC EXPERIENCE: THE PEAK EXPERIENCE

Peakers seem also to live in the realm of Being, of poetry, esthetics, symbols, transcendence, spirituality, of the mystical, personal non-institutional sort.

GEMEINSCHAFTSGEFUHL

They have for human beings in general a deep feeling of identification, sympathy, and affection in spite of the occasional anger, impatience, or disgust. They have a genuine desire to help the human race.

Very few people actually understand them, however much they may like them. However far apart from other people they feel at times, they nevertheless feel a basic underlying kinship with these creatures whom they have to regard with, if not condescension, at least the knowledge that they can do many things better than others can, that they can see things others cannot see, that the truth is as clear to them as it is hidden to others.

INTERPERSONAL RELATIONS

They are capable of more fusion, greater love, more perfect identification, more obliteration of the ego boundaries than other people would consider possible. The other members of these relationships are likely to be healthier and closer to self-actualization than the average. There is high selectiveness here. Their circle of friends is rather small. Devotion is not a matter of a moment but requires a good deal of time and dedication.

Their love of humankind does not lack discrimination. The fact is they can and do speak realistically and harshly of those who deserve it, especially of the hypocritical, the pretentious, the pompous or the self-inflated. Their hostile reactions to others are 1) deserved and 2) for the good of the person attacked or for someone else's good.

Their admirers are apt to demand more than the self-actualized person is willing to give. These devotions can be rather embarrassing, distressing and even distasteful to the self-actualizing individual, since they often go beyond ordinary bounds. The usual picture is of them being kind and pleasant when forced into these relationships, but ordinarily trying to avoid them as gracefully as possible.

DEMOCRATIC CHARACTER STRUCTURE

They can be and are friendly with anyone of suitable character regardless of class, education, political belief, race or colour. As a matter of fact, it seems as if they are not even aware of these differences, which are for the average person so obvious and important.

They find it possible to learn from anybody who has something to teach them, no matter what other characteristics the other person may have. They have a humility of a certain type. These individuals, themselves elite, select their friends from the elite, but it is an elite of character, capacity and talent, rather than of birth, race, blood, family, age, youth, fame or power.

They are more likely rather than less likely to counterattack against evil men and evil behaviour. They are far less ambivalent, confused or weak-willed about their own anger than average people are.

DISCRIMINATION BETWEEN MEANS AND ENDS: BETWEEN GOOD AND EVIL

These individuals are strongly ethical, they have definite moral standards, they do right and do not do wrong. Their notions of right and wrong and of good and evil are often not conventional ones.

 They believe in God but describe God more as a metaphysical concept as a personal figure.

PHILOSOPHICAL UNHOSTILE SENSE OF HUMOR

Characteristically what they consider humor is more closely allied to philosophy than anything else. They do not poke fun at other people's expense.

CREATIVENESS

Each one of them shows in one way or another a special kind of creativeness or originality or inventiveness that has certain peculiar characteristics. These individuals are less inhibited, less constricted, less bound, in a word, less enculturated.

RESISTANCE TO ENCULTURATION; TRANSCENDENCE OF A PARTICULAR CULTURE

They get along with the culture in various ways, but they resist enculturation in a profound and meaningful sense. Their yielding to convention is apt to be rather casual and perfunctory, with cutting corners in favour of directness, honesty, saving energy, etc. In a pinch, when yielding to conventions is too annoying or too expensive, the apparent conventionality reveals itself for the superficial thing it is and tossed of as easily as a cloak.

They are not against fighting but are against ineffective fighting.

DROPPING OF DEFENSES IN LOVE RELATIONSHIPS

They have a tendency to more and more spontaneity, dropping of defenses, dropping of roles and of trying and striving in the relationship. As the relationship continues, there is a growing intimacy and honesty and self-expression, which at its height is a rare phenomenon.

"We can love a person only to the extent that we are not threatened by him; we can love only if his reaction to us or to those things which affect us, are understandable to us."

Sex and love can be and most certainly are perfectly fused with each other in these people.

They can tolerate the absence of sex more easily and will easily give it up, because it came without love and affection.

However, sex can be wholeheartedly enjoyed, far beyond the possibility of the average person, but at the same time it does not play any central role in their philosophy of life. The self-actualizing person can simultaneously enjoy sex so much more intensely than the average person, yet at the same time consider it so much less important in their total frame of reference.

They have an easy relationship with members of the opposite sex, along with the casual acceptance of the phenomenon of being attracted to other people, but at the same time these individuals do rather less about this attraction than other people. Their talk about sex is considerably freer and more casual and unconventional than the average.

Healthier men are more attracted by intelligence, strength, competence in women than threatened by it, as is so often the case with the uncertain male. Self-actualizing women can incorporate their "male qualities" without sacrificing their femininity.

Their love relationships are characterized by fun, merriment, elation, feeling of well-being and gaiety. In spite of the fact that their love lives often reach great peaks of ecstasy, it is also easily compared to the games of children and puppies.

They have the rare ability to be pleased rather than threatened by the partner's triumphs. There is an absence of jealousy.

The self-actualizing person will not casually control or use another or disregard his/her wishes. He/she will allow the respected person a fundamental irreducible dignity and will not unnecessarily humiliate him/her.

Self-actualizing men who tend really to respect and to like women as partners, as equals, as pals are apt to be much easier and freer and familiar and impolite in the traditional sense.

Self-actualizing people's tendencies to detachment and to need identification and to profound interrelationships with another person can coexist within themselves. They have a healthy selfishness, a great self-respect, a disinclination to make sacrifices without good reason. It cannot be said of them that they need each other as ordinary lovers.

They have excellent taste in love and sexual partners. The close friends, husbands and wives of self-actualizing people make a far finer group of human beings than random sampling would indicate.

The people they fall in love with are soundly selected by either cognitive or conative criteria. That is they are intuitively, sexually, impulsively attracted to people who are right for them by cold, intellectual, clinical calculation.

CORTISOL THE DEATHLY STRESS HORMONE

The hypothalamus, part of the limbic system of the brain, is the organ responsible for controlling our hormones. When required, the hypothalamus will send a signal to the glands to produce and release hormones. These hormones are injected into the bloodstream and have receptors all over the body where they dock in. They charge these cells, and change the constitution of that cell. The glands will send a message back to the hypothalamus once satiation stage is reached, and the hypothalamus, working like a thermostat, will turn off production. Hormones that return to the brain, can change the way we think – just imagine a man reading a book and a naked woman passes his line of vision. The rush of dopamine and testosterone will change his thinking. Powerful steroid hormones influence every function in the body, mostly growth in teenagers, metabolism, immune system, etc. It influences men's moods, memory and behaviour.

What happens when Achilles, Aphrodite and a pack of Wild Dogs dance together in the man's body?

Anabolic steroid: Testosterone / Achilles

Testosterone is the magic mojo juice a male runs on. I call testosterone the Achilles of hormones. Imagine Achilles on the verge of charging onto the battlefield; his muscles flexing as he swings his sword, his body tense and taunt, his attention focused on the enemy. He exudes confidence and animal sex appeal. He is fighting fit, aggressive, ready to take enormous risks and on a winning streak. He feels invincible. This is what manhood is all about.

Testosterone causes major changes in Achilles' organs: his bones become denser and his muscle leaner, it increases his haemoglobin to produce clotting agents in his blood to prevent bleeding of wounds. He breathes deeper and faster, promoting oxygen uptake in his blood. His eyes focus only on the enemy directly in front of him. His mood changes to aggression, a sexual predator, prone to sexual fantasies and he is motivated to challenge rivals. Achilles moves with confidence, talks with authority, seeks sex and challenges Hades himself.

Testosterone motivates a man to fight and to win. Imagine Achilles meeting Aphrodite / Dopamine in the nucleus accumbens – the thrill centre of the brain. Winning becomes so thrilling he becomes addicted to it. Even spectators watching their teams win experience an increase in testosterone.

This winning effect reaches beyond the arena of the sports fields, but also to the sales floor, the stock market and even the upper echelons of the business fraternity where multi-billion-dollar deals are clinched.

Cambridge scientists found that when traders' testosterone levels test high in the morning, they make more money on the stock exchange that day. When Brazil beat Italy in the World Cup Final 1994, the average testosterone levels of Brazilian fans increased by 28%, compared to the 27 decrease of the Italian men. A testosterone surge before a competition increases chances of winning and definitely promotes a winning streak. A surge of testosterone after a single victory can last a few months.

Too much...

However, at some point the elevated testosterone levels override the rational neo-cortex. These men begin to believe themselves as invincible, omnipotent, and power giants. They believe they cannot only conquer the world but that they own the world. They sleep less, become more and more driven and their over-confidence pollutes their business relations and leading to disastrous leadership. Alan Greenspan referred to this phenomenon as "irrational exuberance". Women are not prone to the condition as they do not produce the same levels of testosterone as men. In this case, men are more "hormonal" than women!

Too little...

When a testosterone empowered man enters a room, a subordinate male will experience a drop in testosterone and an increase in cortisol, the stress hormone. Cortisol affects the hippocampus, or memory centre as well as other prefrontal cortex functions. The subordinate male will fumble, stumble over his words, act awkwardly and probably have little memory of the social blunders he committed.

When men lose – or their team loses – their testosterone levels plummet.

Achilles bites the dust. Man-down. A drop in testosterone causes irritable male syndrome, they become moody, withdrawn, depressed and miserable. They lack motivation, have low libido, lose interest in sex and in life in general. A remedy would be to get them active, doing things they are good at doing and exposing them to sunshine. Beer is not a good idea, since it contains oestrogen.

Men produce ten times more testosterone than women, but there is a little Achilles in every woman too. Testosterone in men is produced in the testes and adrenals. In women it is produced in the ovaries and adrenals. An enzyme called aromatase can affect testosterone, turning it into the female oestrogen. Fat cells contain aromatase, which is why obese men often grow breasts. This phenomenon is called gynaecomastia.

How fast ...

The time span between the hypothalamus signaling the glands to produce testosterone and the actual effect of it, can take up to fifteen minutes or hours. By age 30 a man's testosterone production begins to decline and he is more rational and cognitive about the risks he is willing to take, than when he was a teenager and his hormones ruled his brain.

How sexy ...

All erotic stimuli – what we see, hear, smell, feel, taste or touch – are first recorded by the thalamus. This triggers a release of dopamine in the nucleus accumbens – the thrill centre. Enter Aphrodite... The hypothalamus sends the signal to release testosterone – enter Achilles. The man will require energy for this venture, so adrenaline is released as well – enter the cheetahs. However, if he is too stressed, - detection of wild dogs - blood will not flow to the male genitals – he needs to be relaxed and in the parasympathetic nervous system, to obtain an erection. (In the sympathetic / stressed nervous system, blood is redirected to the muscles and limbs needed to fight – men do not fight battles with their erections.) To achieve ejaculation, he needs to switch back to the sympathetic nervous system. The cerebellum controls the muscles involved in the contractions, producing the orgasm and this reptile brain activity dampens the prefrontal and temporal higher brain functions, allowing more uninhibited behaviour. An orgasm will release the oxytocin hormone, causing bonding with his partner. Oxytocin releases opiates in the brain, suppressing pain. Sex is good for pain relief.

Catabolic steroid: Cortisol / Wild dogs

Cortisol is the pack of wild dogs released by the gonads. If not kept on leash, they will attack the body from the inside and devour it with ruthless fervour. Initially, when the pack of wild dogs raise their snouts, sniff the wind and jog at a checked steady pace, cortisol, in combination with dopamine, can increase arousal, focus attention and activate a man's senses. It makes him feel alive and alert and full of anticipation.

Cortisol works in conjunction with adrenalin, but the cheetahs soon tire and then the cortisol pack of wild dogs have free range and cause havoc in the man's body. It attacks his digestive system, causing gastric ulcers, stunts growth, and attacks his immune system. It can damage his heart. It raids energy stores, the liver, muscles and fat cells, fervently searching for glucose. It will attack his muscles and turn them into glucose and energy, to feed its wild frenzy. He becomes anxious, paranoid, his memory fails, he becomes over-emotional when his emotional amygdala overrides his rational neo-cortex, and he becomes practically physically and mentally exhausted. It literally causes the dendrites in the brain to shrivel up. Cortisol eats his muscles and his brain.

The lethal combination of cortisol, dopamine and adrenalin cause the conquering warrior effect, but we cannot attempt to conquer Olympus and not anger the gods, so inevitably there follows the spectacular crash and burn. The after effects of the cortisol pack of wild dogs, leave a battlefield scarred with mutilated, ruined men.

Dopamine / Aphrodite

Dopamine is the Aphrodite of the neurotransmitters. She is alluring, she will seduce him and excite him. Dopamine is the anticipation of pleasure and the rewards it promises, she motivates him to move towards that which he desires. She creates euphoria and he becomes addicted to the anticipation, the wanting, the desire, the craving, not necessarily the reward. Dopamine calls him to the hunt and to be excited by the novelty and unexpected pleasure that awaits him. As soon as he becomes used to the reward, the dopamine loses her allure and he becomes bored.

When there is an unexpected reward, the dopamine surge is greater. It is smaller when there is an expected reward. The reward can be anything from sex, securing a major deal, to scoring a goal in sport. Also, when there is an expected disappointment, the dopamine drop is minimal. An unexpected disappointment will cause a major drop in dopamine in the thrill centres of the brain.

Too little dopamine leads to that awful feeling where he has nothing to look forward to. Without dopamine he experiences no pleasure, no motivation and he will stay static. A coach potato man, lying on his back all day watching television, growing fatter and becoming more and more miserable, is a typical example of man lacking dopamine and testosterone.

Aphrodite's danger lies in her addictive powers. She can enslave him. Men can become addicted to winning, to sex, to power as they become addicted to drugs and alcohol.

Too much exposure to dopamine stimuli causes a depletion of dopamine. Too much of a good thing becomes boring. Nothing can excite these men anymore and they take bigger risks, but with less judgement, to experience the euphoria of winning. When that fails, they may fall prey to designer drugs to relieve the boredom and create excitement. Reckless risk-taking leads to mistakes and downfall. This is when they trip over their own ego's. Not every disgraced business tycoon exits on a blaze of glory, they crash and burn on a spectacular level. Achilles paid the price for hubris – he knew he was doomed, and displayed a fatalistic attitude to dangerous risk and died by the arrow of Apollo.

PARENTAL ALIENATION SYNDROME

Please take note that the following should not be construed as legal advice. Please consult with lawyers on these matters. Laws may change and there are different laws applicable in different countries. The following research is added to this book as part of an awareness campaign and not indented by any means as legal advice.

In the 1980's psychiatrist, Dr Richard Gardner first described and identified the concept of Parental Alienation Syndrome, referring to a practice almost exclusively within the context of divorce proceedings, where one parent embarks on a subtle or overt campaign to alienate a child from the other parent. Eventually the child is indoctrinated to such an extent that the child buys into the denigration campaign, avoids the other parent and perceives or believes the other parent to be bad or dangerous. The campaign has no justification, and the alienating parent has no insight into the extensive damage caused to the child, nor does this parent show any guilt or regrets about the behaviour.

Most common behaviour would be for the alienator to block or frustrate the child's contact with the other parent. Examples would be organizing family outings, sleep-overs or play dates during the other parent's weekends, booking expensive luxury holidays for the child during the other parent's vacation time, not being at home at pick-up time, not telling a child that the other parent had called, not answering phones, claiming the child is sleeping or in the bath, or studying when the parent calls, pulling faces when the other parent calls, not informing the other parent of school functions or plays, etc. Reasons given for blocking or frustrating access are usually that the child is unsettled or unruly after visits to the other parent, the child is unsafe, the visits disrupts the child's routine or that the other parent is morally or mentally inferior, whilst the alienator is morally superior. This attitude creates a sense within the child that one parent is better and that the other parent is not equipped to take care of the child. In mild cases the alienator expresses irritation at the inconvenience of the other parent wanting to see the child and in severe cases the alienator expresses: "over my dead body will he / she see the child again."

Some academic literature on the subject:

Gardner's (1999) definition:

"Parental alienation syndrome (PAS, Gardner, <u>1985</u>, <u>1986</u>, <u>1987a</u>, <u>1987b</u>, <u>1989</u>, <u>1992</u>, <u>1998</u>) is a disorder that arises almost exclusively in the context of child-custody disputes. In this disorder, one parent (the alienator, the alienating parent, the PAS-inducing parent) induces a program of denigration against the other parent (the alienated parent, the victim, the denigrated parent)."

PAS implies that the child incorporates the thought patterns and behaviour of the alienating parent towards the absent parent.

Ward & Harvey (1993) on PAS:

"There is a continuum of alienating parental behaviors which cause harm to children, and all positions on this continuum need be of concern to the professionals and the courts. Some of the behavior is scarcely detectable with the result that attorneys and the court system gloss over the alienation as a "normal" part of the divorce or litigation process. However, such barely evident alienating behavior marks the beginning of an alienation continuum.

The Continuum: Differentiating between "Typical" Divorce and "Alienation"

Alienation occurs when a parent uses the child to meet personal emotional needs, as a vehicle to express or carry his/her own intense emotions or as a pawn to manipulate as a way of inflicting retribution on the other side.

Parental alienation occurs along a broad continuum, based on the level of internal distress of the alienating parent, the vulnerability of the child and the responses of the target parent, as well as on the responses of the external system (family, attorneys, mental health professionals, the legal system). The range may be from children who experience significant discomfort at transition times (mild), through children who feel compelled to keep separate worlds and identities when with each parent (moderate); to children who refuse to have anything to do with the target parent and become obsessed with their hatred (severe).

177

Mild

At this stage, despite the seeming sincerity, the alienating parent's view of the other parent is compromised, as indicated by behavior. He/she is not aware of the beliefs and feelings that motivate his/her unintentional alienating behavior (internal) or of the effect that statements and behavior can have on the child (interactional).

Because the statements of the alienating parent will not give the lawyers or the courts clues that there is alienation in process, it is important to look at the underlying messages that are given directly to the child. The communications to the child of the regard with which the other parent is held is the key to detecting alienating behavior.

Moderate

The alienating parent has some awareness of emotional motivations (fear of loss, rage) and little sense of the value of the target parent. Sometimes, an alienating parent will understand the theoretical importance of the other parent in the life of the child, but believes that in this case, the other parent, due to character deficiencies, cannot be important to the child. Their statements and behaviors are subtle but damaging to the child.

Overt

When the alienation is overt, the motivation to alienate, the intense hatred of the other, is blatant. The alienating parent is obsessed and sees the target as noxious to self, the children, and even the world. A history of the marriage reflects nothing but the bad times. The target parent was never worthwhile as a spouse or a parent and is not worthwhile today. Such a parent shows little response to logic and little ability to confront reality.

Many alienating parents at this stage entertain the overt belief that the target parent presents an actual danger of harm to the children. They present this belief as concrete knowledge that if the children spend time with the target parent they will be harmed in some manner.

Severe

By the severe stage, the alienating parent no longer needs to be active. In terms of the motivation, the alienating parent holds no value at all for the other parent; the hatred and disdain are overt. The alienating parent will do anything to keep the children away from the target parent.

At this stage the child is enmeshed with the alienating parent and takes on the alienating parent's desires, emotions and hatreds and verbalizes them to all as his own. The child too believes that the target parent is a villain and the scum of the earth and sees the history of the target parent and family as all negative. The child is neither able to remember nor express any positive feeling for the target parent.

"Weapons" are the false allegations by the alienating parent of behavior on the part of the target parent inimicable to the welfare of a child. The most commonly used weapons are false allegations of:

threats of or actual domestic violence;
sexual abuse of the child;
physical abuse of the child;
emotional abuse of the child;
mental illness on the part of the target parent;
alcoholism/drug abuse/homosexuality on the part of the target parent; or
threats of moving or flight by the alienating parent.

If it is unclear that there is in fact abuse (sexual or physical), then the allegations may have been produced by the intensity of feelings about the divorce, fear of abuse and a misreading of particular situation. However, muddled the waters are, the court must establish a factual basis upon which to proceed legally (either abuse did or did not occur) or the system will be paralyzed to the advantage of the alienating parent. Unless disproven, the allegations will cast a pall of potential harm to the child that no one person, institution or agency will be able to ignore, and an accused will always be treated as guilty unless proven innocent with regards to contact with the children."

Rand (1997) on "brainwashing":

"Brainwashing" was defined as the interactional process by which the child was persuaded to accept and elaborate on the program. Brainwashing occurs over time and involves repetition of the program, or code words referring to the program, until the subject responds with attitudinal and behavioural compliance. According to Clawar and Rivlin, the influence of a programming parent can be conscious and wilful or unconscious and unintentional. It can be obvious or subtle, with rewards for compliance that were material, social or psychological. Noncompliance may be met with subtle psychological punishment such as withdrawal of love or direct corporal punishment.

Some cases of PAS, especially those with false allegations of abuse, may have important features in common with Munchausen Syndrome by Proxy (MSP) in which parents fulfil their needs vicariously by presenting their child as ill. In cases of classical MSP, parents repeatedly take their children to doctors unnecessarily, often painful tests and treatments which the physician is induced to provide, based on the parent's misrepresentations. "Contemporary type MSP" occurs when a parent fabricates an abuse scenario for the child and welcomes or actively seeks out repeated abuse interviews of the child by police, social workers and therapists.

The concept of contemporary-type MSP elaborates on the idea put forth by Sinanan and Houghton that new types of MSP behaviour will evolve in parallel with the evolution of new medical and social services, eg. the child protection system. MSP parents may change or come up with new "symptoms" for the child as to better elicit the desired response from a particular care provider or an institution offering specialised services. Thus, the same child may be receiving attention simultaneously for fabricated physical symptoms from several medical providers and for fabricated sex abuse from therapists and public agencies who specialise in abuse. Careful evaluation and thorough investigation of sex abuse allegations which turn out to be questionable or false will sometimes bring a parent to the attention of authorities for practicing "classical" as well as "contemporary-type" MSP."

Warshak (2001) on PAS:

"In some cases of moderate PAS, when the parent is more intensively programming the children and there is a high risk of the alienation becoming more severe, Gardner recommends a different legal approach. In such cases he recommends courts consider awarding primary custody to the alienated parent and extremely restricted contact between the alienating parent and child, in order to prevent further indoctrination. Similarly, in the most severe cases of PAS (which in Gardner's experience, comprise about 5 – 10 percent of all PAS cases) Gardner recommends that the court remove the children from the alienating parent.

The importance of separating the child from the alienating parent, ensuring the child's exposure to the target parent, is consistent with treatment methods for victims of brainwashing, including prisoners of war and members of cults... "One of the most powerful tools the courts have is the threat and implementation of environmental modification. Of the approximately four hundred cases we have seen where the courts increased the contact with the targeted parent... there has been positive change in 90 percent of the relationships between the child and the target parent, including the elimination or reduction of many socio-psychological, educational and physical problems that the child presented prior to the modification."

Bone and Walsh (1999) on PAS:

A marked deterioration in the relationship between the child and the absent parent. A previously healthy relationship will not rapidly deteriorate. On the contrary children miss the absent parent and usually cannot wait to see him / her. Normal healthy relationships do not erode easily, despite the parent's absence. A rapid deterioration indicates the alienator has been poisoning the mind of the child against the other parent. Children eventually voice abuse against the estranged parent because they fear the wrath of the alienating parent. They know they face disapproval or even punishment should they contact, side or even express that they miss or would want to see the estranged parent.

The alienating parent usually has a controlling "my way or the highway" attitude. When children misbehave, they are accused of being "just as useless as your father / stupid as your mother." They alienating parent also manipulates the child to feel guilty for leaving "your sick mother at home", or "remember I love you more", or "remember I am waiting all weekend for you to return and I know you are going to miss me as much as I miss you", etc. Especially young children fear that they will be abandoned by the primary care-giver, if they dare to visit the estranged parent. The alienating parent refuses to attend sport or cultural activities if the other parent is going to be there, the child is not allowed to have photographs of the alienated parent nor to mention the parent's name or family.

The impact of PAS on the child:

Gardner (1999):

"PAS Parents who induce PAS in their children are often oblivious to the psychologically detrimental effects of the progressive attenuation of the child's bond with the target parent. In extreme cases it appears that the alienating parent would be pleased if the alienated parent were to evaporate from the face of the earth--making sure, beforehand, to bequeath an annuity for the remaining family. Such alienators basically believe that absolutely nothing would be lost to the children under such circumstances."

Read Richard Gardner's article on Differentiating between Parental Alienation Syndrome and bona fide abuse neglect in The American Journal of Family Therapy, vol 27,no 2 p 97 – 107, April – June 1999.

Ward & Harvey (1993):

"There are three underlying premises regarding the development of children that underlie this article. First, all litigation concerning children can affect their healthy growth and development negatively. The greater the acrimony and the greater the part that the children need or are asked to play in the litigation, the greater the potential for harm.(2) "[T]he persistent quality of the conflict combined with its enduring nature seriously endangers the mental health of the parents and the psychological development of the children. Under the guise of fighting for the child, the parents may succeed in inflicting severe emotional suffering on the very person whose protection and well-being is the presumed rationale for the battle." Johnston, J.R. B Campbell, L.E.G., Impasses of Divorce "Forward" by J. Wallerstein, p.ix (1988).

Second, it is psychologically harmful to children to be deprived of a healthy relationship with one parent. There is a substantial body of research that indicates that children need contact with adults of both sexes for balanced development."(3)

Third, with the exception of abuse, there is no good reason why children should not want to spend some time with each of their parents, and, even with abuse, most children still want to maintain some relationship with the abusive parent. It is the job of the parents, the professionals and the courts to see that such contact is possible under safe circumstances.(4)

Alienating messages and behaviour, whether intentional or not, place the child in a severe loyalty bind, a position wherein the child believes she must choose which of her two parents she will "love" more. To have to choose between parents is itself damaging to the child, and, if the end result is the exclusion of a parent from the child's life, the injury is irreparable."

Rand (1997):

"Gardner was among the first to recognize that involving a child in false allegations of abuse is a form of abuse in itself and indicative of serious problems somewhere in the divorce family system.

Cartwright poignantly describes the psychological effects on the child of being involved in severe PAS. "The child experiences a great loss, the magnitude of which is akin to the death of a parent, two grandparents, and all the lost parent's relatives and friends ... Moreover... the child is unable to acknowledge the loss, much less mourn it. The child's good memories of the alienated parent are systematically destroyed, and the child misses out on the day-to-day interaction, learning, support and love, which, in an intact family, usually flows between the child and both parents, as well as grandparents and relatives on both sides. The child may encounter insurmountable obstacles if, later in life, he or she seeks to re-establish relations with the lost parent and his family. The lost parent may be unwilling to become reinvolved. The parent or grandparents may have died. Some of these children eventually turn against the alienating parent, and if the target parent is lost to them as a child, the child is left with an unfillable void."

Johnston (2001):

"Alienated children are likely to be controlling, distrustful and easily disillusioned. They enter into therapy, often reluctantly, with a scripted story and a demand for the therapists' immediate allegiance to their position. The child's challenge is "Are you for me, or are you against me?" The therapist is placed in a bind - the cost of a therapeutic alliance with the child appears to require the sacrifice of his or her therapeutic objectivity. Moreover, the therapist remains on trial - any hint of subsequent disloyalty threatens to precipitate his or her dismissal by the child...A feature of alienated children is their bland, stripped-down and simplistic black/white thinking and poor reality testing."

Warshak (2003):

"Irrationally alienated children harbor hatred for a parent that is dissociated from their earlier love for that parent. Their internal mental state has a rift that cannot heal until it is acknowledged.

Adults who have truly suffered at the hands of inadequate parents and subsequently resolved their feelings are able to express a wide range of feelings about their parents... this is something a pathologically alienated person is unable to do, and it handicaps them in their most personal relationships.

A man who is out of touch with his loving feelings for his father has more difficulty promoting the highest-quality loving relationship with his own children;

A man who cannot appreciate the importance of his father in his life and of what he loses by not having a father, has more difficulty appreciating his own importance in his children's lives;

184

A man who cuts himself off from his own feelings is less sensitive to the feelings of his wife and children;

A man who has no contact with his father and extended family deprives his own children of a grandparent and his wife of the support available through the extended family.

The saddest consequence of divorce poison occurs when a rejected parent or grandparent dies before the child has come to his/her senses, given his/her love, apologized for his/her mistreatment and expressed regret for the lost years. It is at this point that a child is most apt to resent the brainwashing parent whose efforts deprived the child of a relationship that cannot be recaptured.

When alienated children, as adults, eventually realize what they have missed out on and the immense magnitude of the hurt their behaviour has caused their loved ones, they suffer unbearable guilt and sadness. This suffering has a direct effect on their marriage and their children…If children of divorce are more likely to end a marriage rather than work out conflicts, this risk is multiplied for children who have totally rejected a parent."

Hillaker (2010):

Early identification of a child suffering from PAS can diminish a child's psychological damage. Early identification will allow a child to recover their true relationship with the targeted parent. There is a point of no return for the child psychologically. Enough psychological damage can be done to the child wherein the child may never recover from the indoctrination of falsehoods and vilification of the targeted parent. Early identification and treatment diminish the harm caused psychologically to their child and the targeted parent. PAS primarily manifests itself in divorce and family separation cases.

The younger the child, the more severe the psychological damage can be to the child, if PAS is not identified and treated early.

"A secondary syndrome in divorce that has emerged in the last twenty years is Sexual Allegations In Divorce (SAID)… Austin also claims that the false allegations coupled with leading questions or suggestive counselling result in children: developing false memories; being fatherless; becoming depressed; becoming suicidal, losing self-esteem (www.falseallegations.com/parental.html.) ... Children who have been subconsciously engaged in SAID and PAS may engage in acting out behaviours in adolescents and early adulthood and have psychological problems for a life time.

Introducing PAS to child is a form of emotional child abuse. Emotional abuse is of course psychological abuse, which can be more damaging than physical abuse. When the child grows up, they may not realize what actually happened, and how PAS affected them and the alienated parent psychologically. The PAS child/adult may have lifelong psychological problems. Children may not be able to outgrow their own pain and the humiliation they experienced as a PAS child. If PAS existed for a long period of time between the PAS child and the alienated parent, the PAS child may experience lifelong psychological problems. PAS children who have experienced PAS more than likely will have relationship problems with other children, significant others, and in their private and professional peer group. The normal bond and psychological attachments between a PAS child and their parent has been altered and possibly destroyed.

The PAS child, now an adult, will have a relationship between the alienating parent and the alienated parent. If that PAS child/adult can recognize previous PAS issues in their prior relationships, it may put them on a recovery path, to discover what actually happened to them in their childhood. Childhood memories of family dynamics, of pre and post family separation can be fluid and disposed of memory errors. Though the child will have varying memories, their true memories may never come out. The only mental health answer is therapy."

A common criticism against PAS is since it is not categorised in the Diagnostic Statistical Manual (textbook for psychologists and psychiatrists) it does not exist. In 2010 I testified in a court case in South Africa where the Honourable Judge Claasen found that it did exist and after my testimony he ordered that the boy be removed from his mother and placed in the care of his father that very same day.

THE S.A.I.D. (SEXUAL ALLEGATIONS IN DIVORCE) SYNDROME:

Another abhorrence that rises its ugly head in divorce cases is when one parent makes false allegations that a child has been sexually abused by the other parent.

Blush & Ross (1986) on SAID:

"This acronym describes the particular phenomenon which occurs when a sexual abuse allegation develops within a pre- or post-divorce context and when a family unit has become dysfunctional as a result of the divorce process.

"it is true that children have imaginations and that they sometimes lie, as do adults, but it is a very uncommon occurrence for a child to fantasize or make up a sexual assault incident... Observe physical and behavioural signs... extreme changes in behaviour such as loss of appetite. Recurrent nightmares... and fear of the dark. Regression to more infantile behaviour such as bedwetting, thumb sucking or excessive crying... Fear of a person or an intense dislike at being left somewhere or with someone. Other behavioural signals such as aggressive or disruptive behaviour, withdrawal, running away or delinquent behaviour, failing in school.

Information source after information source being presented by various social and health organizations take on this common message format.

The hazard in these instructional messages is that over generalized statements concerning behavioural signs, which may mean sexual abuse, can just as realistically be symptomatic of any number of other problems occurring in a child's life. Divorce, peer problems, school related problems, and general developmental processes are all equally competing clinical hypotheses for such behaviours and should be treated as such in investigative stages."

Typical pattern:

Background:

The allegation almost always surfaces only after separation and legal action between the parents has begun

There is a history of family dysfunction with resultant unresolved divorce conflict. This usually involves "hidden' underlying issues both spoken and unspoken

There are often unresolved visitation or custody problems

There are often unresolved money issues relating to the divorce

Personality Profile of the Presenting Parent – Female:

The personality pattern of the female parent often tends to be that of a hysterical personality

She often presents herself as a fearful person who believes she has been the victim of manipulation, coercion, and physical, social or sexual abuse in the marriage

She also tends to see the man as being a source of physical threat, economic punitiveness and retribution, or an individual who simply has not understood the physical safety and psychological needs of the children

She is also often the "justified vindicator", a hostile, emotionally expansive, vindictive, and dominant female who has directly appealed to "experts" in both the mental and health and/or legal communities. She frequently insists on formal punitive legal measures be taken via prosecution before reasonable proofs have been demonstrated. She will often have concurrent criminal action pending with her domestic legal action.

Another personality pattern which requires clinical consideration is when the reporting adult is possibly psychotic.

Conclusion: Regardless of whether the female pattern has been that of the passive, fearful, apprehensive individual, the "justified vindicator", or even that of the psychotic, she is emotionally convinced of the "facts" and will not be dissuaded from her perceptions. The intensity with which she relates to the world through her emotions significantly overshadows her use of a rational reasoning or problem-solving approach to the situation. This emotional appeal can become convincing and very misleading to the inexperienced and/or "well-intended" professional.

Personality Profile of the Presenting Parent – Male:

He is often intellectually rigid, has a high need to be "correct".

He has been hypercritical of the mother throughout the marriage and verbalizes in a number of "nit-picking" ways the suspicion that she has been a non-vigilant and borderline unfit mother.

He typically makes allegations more against the males with whom she has become involved rather than necessarily making direct allegations toward her as the actual perpetrator of the sexual abuse. The male sees her as the person whose passive or silent endorsement of the perpetrator is her contribution to that situation.

He also makes statements about the frequency with which she leaves the children unsupervised, in the care of incompetent or inappropriate babysitters, or generally "at risk" in the home.

Personality Profile of the Alleged Perpetrator – Male:

He is an inadequate personality with marked passive and dependent features.

He presents a socially naive perception of the adult world.

He initially takes a "caretaker" role toward the female during courtship and the early stages of marriage.

He needs to "earn" love by yielding to the wants and demands of the spouse.

Because of these dynamics, it is this type of male who typically finds himself in a relationship with a more dominant female, regardless of whether her dominance is due to emotional hysteria or self-centeredness and vindictiveness.

Personality Profile of the Child

The child has a limited verbal ability with which to articulate their own agenda

The child's immaturity causes him/her to be unable to test and comprehend the reality of the situation in which he/she finds him-/herself, ie the politics of adult divorce

The child is often a female under the age of eight who controls the situation. Additionally, this child may show behavioural patterns of verbal exaggerations, excessive willingness to indict, inappropriate affective responses, and inconsistencies in relating the incident (s).

The child's responses appear to be coached or rehearsed

The child spontaneously initiates conversation during interview by quoting the same phrases accompanied with the same affect as did the controlling parent who presented the complaint

The child uses age-inappropriate verbal descriptions with no demonstrated practical comprehension of what they were saying

The child offers a spontaneous and automatic reporting of the act (s) perpetrated upon them in the absence of any direct questions soliciting this specific information

The child offers inconsistencies in various aspects of reported incidents. These variances may involve specifics (who, what, where, when); frequency (only once or twice, exaggerated to many times); and subjective perceptual experiences (very frightened, not scared, hurt, not hurt, etc)

The child lacks the appearance of a traumatized individual both emotionally and behaviourally.

As children approach adolescence, they develop a more vindictive agenda, and they often speak in absolutes with exaggerated emotional content. The basic agenda is one of not getting their own way, or the other parent has been imposing limits which the adolescent disagrees with.

The allegation is first communicated via the custodial parent, usually the mother

The mother takes the child to an "expert" for further examination, assessment or treatment

The expert then often communicates to a court or other appropriate authorities a concern and/or "confirmation" of apparent sexual abuse, usually identifying the father as the alleged perpetrator

This typically causes the court to react to the "expert's" information by acting in a predictably responsible manner, eg suspending or terminating visitation, foreclosing on custodial arguments, or in some way limiting the child-parent interaction.

The professional as Potential Victim of S.A.I.D. Syndrome:

All too often, the intervening professional sees the case on a preliminary basis in a limited and biased perspective and frequently responds to the presenting parent's report rather than viewing the situation as part of the family's marital and divorce conflict.

Too often the therapeutic community accepts this "presenting process" and creates a clinical focus on assumed trauma and thus the need for immediate treatment of the child.

This process of accepting a presenting complaint as valid and truthful without sophisticated inquiry or clinical challenge creates the vulnerable expert opinion.

Once the initial distortions are communicated by an expert and reinforced through further contacts with the child and/or other involved adults, "facts" are created which then shape the outcome of the situation. This can occur to such a degree that the presenting parent, the child, the therapist, social and legal agencies, and any other involved persons accept this "created reality" that has become the truth.

Experience in the field investigation and follow-up of SAID cases reveals that the therapist is reluctant to change his/her perception once their professional opinion has been formulated.

A further concern is that the clinical focus has been so heavily predicated upon the belief that "children do not lie" so as to make any other considerations secondary.

The ignoring of other information is often justified in the name of "saving" the child from permanent traumatic damage.

It is ironic it is that the intervention agent or therapist who misdiagnoses a SAID case literally creates a scenario from which the family may never recover. This damage, once done, will, in our opinion, perpetuate itself throughout the rest of the history of the family. It may only partially be undone through skillful intervention of a qualified family therapist who, under the most difficult of circumstances, may bring the family members together and help them understand the dynamics of how the SAID phenomenon occurred.

Conclusion: A proper investigation/evaluation in which the collection of collateral information, background information, awareness of conflict, unresolved issues in the divorce is of the utmost importance.

Please read more:

www.skepticfiles.org/conspire/said.html Blush, GJ & Ross, KL 1986. Sexual allegations in divorce, the SAID syndrome.

Blush, Gordon J & Ross, Karol L (1986), Sexual Allegations in Divorce, The S.A.I.D Syndrome,

Cowling, A, The S.A.I.D. Syndrome, Sexual Allegations in Divorce.

Bone, J.M. & Walsh, M.R. 1999. Parental Alienation Syndrome: How to detect it and what to do about it. The Florida Bar Journal, vol 73, no 3, March 1999, p 44-48.

Gardner, RA 1999. Differentiating between parental alienation syndrome and bona-fide abuse-neglect. The American Journal of Family Therapy, (27)2 p 97 – 107

www.hillakerinvestigations.com/2010/05/: Identification of Parental Alienation Syndrome (PAS) and Sexual Allegations in Divorce (SAID) and Child Custody Evaluations: An investigative Literature Review.

Holman WD, 1998. The Fatherbook: A document for Therapeutic work with father-absent early adolescent boys. Child and Adolescent Social Work Journal (15) 2.

Johnston, JR. 2001. Rethinking parental alienation and redesigning parentchild access services for children who resist or refuse visitation. Administration of Justice Department, San Jose State University.

Rand, DC 1997. The Spectrum of Parental Alienation Syndrome. American Journal of Forensic Psychology. (15) 3

Warshak, RA 2001. Current controversies regarding parental alienation syndrome. American Journal of Forensic Psychology. (19) 3

Warshak, RA 2003. Divorce Poison. New York: Harper

Ward, P & Harvey JC 1993. Family Wars: Aienation of Children. New Hampshire Bar Journal (34)1.

WELCOME TO LIFE AS A SINGLE INDEPENDENT WOMAN

So, you're newly divorced, never want to marry or date again and decide it is time to become that wonderful vision of a Single Independent Woman owning your own house? No more little Cinderella-waiting-for-the-prince for you. Here are some pointers to becoming a Single Independent Woman, from one who has done this for decades:

Do you realise when you buy your own house that besides the transfer costs, lawyer's costs, insurance and all the other hidden costs, you have to consider the following:

Do you realise shopping will never be the same again? From now on hardware stores take preference over Woolies, shoe shops and boutiques. Tools and especially power tools, top your birthday present wish list, and believe me, you appreciate these much more than another bottle of bubble bath, especially if is lavender flavour.

Do you know you have to replace the batteries of the electric fence and alarm systems – so they remain activated when there is a power failure. Do you even know where these alarms are and how they work? Do you know if you have five remotes it will cost you a fortune to replace all and have all of them calibrated again, even if you lose just one? A handyman has to come to your house to calibrate them all again. Remember to replace the remotes' batteries.

If the previous owners rewired the bar fridge themselves, you cannot get a normal electrician to fix it, it has to be a refrigerator man because it involves gas. Here is a tip, look on the fridge for the manufacturer's telephone number instead of paging through the yellow pages. Take his (and all other handymen's) personal cell numbers, for often enough you have to call them back for a job half-done.

The electric cable of your electric garage door runs in a shaft and this needs to be greased regularly or the motor will burn out. Did you know that you need a special grease called Brana grease and that you cannot use normal car grease as it erodes the whole thing? You would have to pay to degrease it if you used the wrong grease and reinstall the remote. You cannot get Brana at hardware stores, only at manufacturers of garage door motors.

Do you know to replace that little fan belt of the electric garage door shaft costs a fortune because it is imported? Do you know you would not have to replace it if you used the right grease? It is still cheaper than buying a new motor.

Do you know if you do not secure your electric gate motor with a huge round padlock costing a fortune then thieves will unscrew the motor and steal it? A new motor costs another fortune, and you can claim this motor back from the house-insurance at the bank, but you will pay for the vat and anti-theft bracket, which will cost you a fortune plus another fortune for the padlock and you have to take the day off work to go to the police station to make the statement about the theft before you can claim the insurance and you have to take another day off work and be at home when they install the new motor. So just buy the padlock for the fortune from the beginning.

Do you realise you do not have a husband who can do all of this for you and there is no-one at home when you arrive after dark who could have switched on the lights, checked the pool's Creepy Crawly and the filters, changed the light bulbs, fed the cat and started dinner. If you arrive after sunset – you arrive at a dark house, an annoyed cat and risk being hi-jacked in your driveway.

Do you have your Security Company and Mr Delivery take-away's numbers on speed dial on your phone? Some security companies are kind enough to wait for you in your driveway if you give them a call on your way home, but they won't feed the cat.

Do you know you better stop for milk, bread and cold drink on your way home, for there is no secretary, no husband, housekeeper and no flat mate etc. to buy this for you and your cat doesn't do groceries. Do you know that Mr Delivery can deliver milk and cold drink, even alcohol as well, but not cat food?

Do you know if you do not regularly clean all three filters of the swimming pool and check the Creepy Crawly's throat for pebbles, the motor can burn out and a new Creepy Crawly costs a fortune? Regular means every other day, so this is another reason why you want to be home before sunset. If the creepy is not working, clean the filters, check if a section in the pipe has a hole in it and replace only that section or replace the big round rubber flap instead of buying a new Creepy. I fixed a hole in the creepy with Pratley Putty – silicone doesn't work.

Do you know once you made it home before sunset, attended to the garage door that makes an awful noise and refuses to close (if the springs on the side are worn out, they can be adjusted with a screwdriver instead of replacing them), checked the Creepy in the pool, changed the broken light bulbs, fed the cat and switched on the alarm system, you are allowed to watch soaps on television without disturbance and without answering your cell phone or feeling guilty about it. This is why you became single in the first place, right?

Do you realise when you get up in the middle of the night due to a strange noise and you have to check the property for burglars with a weapon in one hand and cell phone in the other and the car - and house keys dangling in between your fingers, that it is better to wear a dressing gown / track suit with pockets and not do this dressed in your underwear, shortie pajamas and bunny slippers, especially if you live next to a student commune or across a men's hostel like I used to do.

Do you know if the previous owners rewired the irrigation system themselves, you have to have it rewired and have your lawn dug up in the process? And these guys are most likely to puncture a water pipe or the pool, as in my case.

Do you know if you have wooden floors it will cost you a fortune to have the termites checked and killed? If you ask nicely, they will do the lawn for you as well, but this does not kill big black ants.

Can you prune the roses, de-weed the garden and mow your own lawn without killing yourself? Do you own a lawnmower, weed-eater, garden hose, wheelbarrow, shears and garden tools?

Do you have a friend who is a fundi on computers? Get one. Anti-virus programmes need to be updated annually.

Do you know even a simple job such as changing a light bulb is a major effort? I had high ceilings and had to buy one of those fancy ladders that fold open, because there is no-one to hold a normal ladder for me. Also, even the fancy ladder is so damn tight and difficult to open that I regularly break my nails. Spray-n-cook is not a good replacement for oil, no matter what people say.

Do you know that a woman's hand is too small to open the anti-child proof swimming pool pod and that you can hold the bottle between your knees and struggle till you open it, but don't do it with your teeth because it is poisonous. Also, you will hurt your hand and break your fingernails every time you switch the pool motor from filter, to backwash, to rinse and when you clean that inside filter, so don't expect not to get hurt.

Can you take your pool's temperature and administer the right medicine if it is green after a thunderstorm?

Do you also strew lawn feed on your lawn during a thunderstorm, because if the chemicals don't get enough water very soon, they will burn the grass? Wear a raincoat and no bunny slippers when you do this.

Can you make a decent fire in the fireplace and have you discovered firelighters? Do your friends laugh when you add a bag of firewood to your birthday present wish list?

Do you know that it is your responsibility to check when your driver's license expires and that you have to take a day of work to stand in the queue to have it renewed and what it will cost you? Do you know they don't accept colour photos although it says so on the notice boards, so you have to take off another day from work and come back the following day?

Do you check when your passport expires? What about your firearm license?

Do you know how much it costs you to have a vehicle registered on your name and you still need to pay the insurance monthly?

Do you know you have to ask your vehicle tracking company to check you car every six months, else your insurance is invalid and they won't pay out – check the small print.

Do you know besides checking oil, water and petrol you also have to check brake fluid and if the brake fluid is empty (and you have no brakes) you can't just buy a bottle and pour it in, your brakes have to be bled by a professional. I don't know how much this costs, but I have a friend who did it for me.

Do you take your car for regular services every 15 000 km as the booklet advises? You should. Your husband used to do this for you. You have to first phone the garage and make an appointment. Then you drive to the garage before 08h00 and hand in the car and the keys. Then get a cup of coffee, sit down and wait for one of the drivers to take you home or to your work. The same driver will fetch you at about 5 o'clock and make sure you have your credit card ready. At least your car is washed when you fetch it, because who has time to wash it?

Do you know the number of a tow-in service or do you have such a sticker on your car?

Do you know that you are not allowed to touch those long-shaped light bulbs/globes for the spotlights with your bare fingers and you have to use a clean rag, whilst balancing on the stepladder and biting the star screwdriver between your teeth? Don't get up there with a normal flat screwdriver, you are just going to have to get down again and fetch a star screwdriver. You do know the difference, don't you? If you lose (or accidently swallow) the screw, you can use one of those black plastic tie-thingies, but then you have to climb the ladder with the globe (held in a clean rag), scissors to cut the old black tie-thingie and a spare black tie-thingie all in your hands and beware that the glass pane does not slip out, because the rubber around it disintegrates, faster than cheese go bad in your fridge.

Do you know your house's gutters have to be cleaned once a year before the rain season, at least? Invest in that ladder and plastic gloves.

Do you know the wooden window frames that look so expensive and all other wood have to be treated at least once every six months, else they will rot and that they are very expensive to replace?

Are you on first name terms with the shop assistants at the hardware store? Do you have a fully equipped toolbox, and do you know you can get a fixture for screws, which fits on your electric drill like a bit and you don't have to buy an electric screwdriver? You don't have to have an electric screwdriver of course, but stock up on band-aids and expect tough blisters on your hands, if you don't. Also invest in a Hilti.

Do you know a tube of silicone can fix the leak in your shower top, plug up a leak in the irrigation system and seal a hole in your roof? You can also get rubber stick-on strips to seal window frames from drafts.

Do you have your own lawyer, financial adviser, personal banker and auditor? Get them and remember their birthdays. Do you have a retirement plan and do you pay through your nose for premiums and would you rather eat sardines for a month than skip any of these payments, for you are now a single income family – you and your cat – and there is no second income salary or hubby to take care of you when you are old and decrepit?

Do you have a medical aid fund that costs you a fortune per month and do you have Professional Income Protection for if you dare to get sick and you are self-employed, there is nobody to earn money to pay the bills at the end of the month and buy the cat's food? You may send yourself flowers if you are sick and you can afford it.

Can you fill in a tax form? Do you keep all your slips, invoices etc and file them for your auditor and hand it in just after end of February?

Can you pay your accounts on the Internet and do you have all the security requirements updated as stipulated by the bank? Do you know about pin codes, passwords and extra security and do you check your bank statements every month, including cheque, credit, car, house bond, savings etc? Come again… savings – you think you can save? You've got be kidding!

Do you remember to refill the big gas bottle for the gas barbeque and make sure the gardener is there that day, for how the dickens do you think are you going to manage to off load that thing on your own? Keep the slip for the refill and remember to turn off the gas when you have finished the barbeque or become a vegetarian like me and leave the barbeque for your male friends.

A new tyre for your car costs a fortune or more and remember to stand in the queue again to renew your car registration every year, because they no longer send you reminders.

Do you remember your cell phone contract needs to be updated every two years and you need to take another day off work to do this?

If you ever think of DIY building, rather shoot yourself in the knee or chew off your left breast. It is less agonizing.

Do you have a contract for the tenant? Who fixes the geyser? Do you know that you cannot use a domestic violence interdict against a paying in-house tenant and an eviction order will cost you thousands and take months, so you have to screen very carefully whom you allow to live in your house? Beware of legal-wise old ladies, who work on your sympathy, move in with their dogs, drive into your car and cost you a fortune to evict. Check with your lawyer.

Do you know if someone shares your house and you do not charge him/her rent (and you have proved it with receipts, even if it is a minimum amount per month), they can claim a domestic relationship and move out with all your furniture, although you bought everything? This includes husbands, boyfriends, relatives and friends. Draw up a contract or get one at a stationary store. Check with your lawyer.

Can you replace a windowpane, putty and all? Can you replace a door lock, fix a leaking faucet and replace a floor tile?

Do you know the value of Clean Green?

Do you remember to put the garbage bin out on the evening before collections or else you have to do it early that morning, even though you are all prettily dressed up for work and smell like garbage once you have done it? Do you know they don't remove garbage bags placed next to the bin? The bags have to be inside. And these guys still have the audacity to ask for Christmas boxes!

If your tv/ decoder blinks out, do you have your smart card number, do you know where the smart card is in the decoder and can you actually get a picture back on the screen without having to phone the emergency number, because everyone is phoning that number right then and you are going to wait in a long queue and miss your soaps. PS you should be watching international news – not soaps. You need to make an impression as an intelligent well-informed woman at that next dinner party and not sound like a spoiled housewife hooked on soaps.

Do you know where to take your decoder for an upgrade?

Do you realise if you work a full week you have no time to buy, fix, change and exchange all these things during the week and therefore you never get to tan next to your beautiful sparkling pool, because you spend the whole damn weekend driving around and fixing things.

Do you realise at least once a year, you deserve a hot rock massage? Forget the manicure – you have no nails left.

Wouldn't it be nice if someone opens a pub and install laundry machines and tumble dryers, so single women can have a drink, relax and get their laundry done on a Friday after work? Then we might have time to watch International News programmes on Sunday evenings and sound clever at work on Monday mornings.

Do you realise despite all this, you hope you have an understanding boss who does not expect you to work after dark; a regular salary increase; gay friends who double up as handymen and do not expect sex as payment; a sense of humor and in the end you still like to be a Single Independent Woman, because there is nothing like watching television at six o clock in the evening, bathed and dressed up in your Garfield jammies and bunny slippers, eating whatever you feel like and not having to please the whole family. Except of course your cat, who thinks you are the cat's whiskers, because he just got fed that scrumptious imported expensive cat food, which you remembered to buy on your way home. Congratulations!

PS: If you happen to be a husband reading this, show it to your wife and she might appreciate you more. I know I would appreciate it.

DISCIPLINE PROTOCOL FOR CHILDREN

DR PISTORIUS' PROTOCOL FOR DESIRED BEHAVIOUR

All parents have a responsibility to bring up their children to become law-abiding, contributing and productive citizens of a country.

Parents often make the common mistake of asking a child why he/she has done something wrong and the standard answer is always: "I don't know." Parents should rather ask the children what the consequences of their actions are, and if they answer they don't know, give them one or two hints, and then encourage them to come up with at least one or two consequences themselves.

Children are very impulsive and especially young children do not appreciate the consequences of their actions, as their prefrontal cortex' have not yet developed to execute this function. They should be taught from a young age that every action has long-term and short-term consequences. For example, the long-term consequences of smoking marijuana would be that the guilty person can acquire a criminal record and would therefore never be able to acquire a work or travel visa to another country. Unprotected sex can lead to sexually transmitted diseases, AIDS and pregnancy. Encouraging them to consider and verbally express the consequences of actions, will teach them to think twice before they repeat misbehaviour and it will teach them to become responsible adults.

There is a difference between discipline and punishment.

Discipline refers to good manners, maintaining a clean, orderly and hygienic environment, sticking to schedules, etc. and thus teaching the child to acquire self-discipline. Self-discipline is a healthy habit, which makes interpersonal relations during adulthood easier. Parents may indulge children's bad table manners, tardiness or untidy rooms, but future colleagues, employers, friends, flat mates and life partners will not, and this can lead to interpersonal conflict. No-one likes a person who thinks the world owes him/her something and who expects other people to clean up after them or accommodate their bad habits.

Punishment is the consequence of an offence. Just as a country has a judicial system differentiating between civil and criminal offences, so the judicial system within a household should distinguish between these two elements.

Children do not like rules at home, nor in school. Explain to them that even as adults we are bound by rules and laws and since there is absolutely no escaping this anywhere on the planet, the sooner we learn to abide, the less trouble we get in and the better we get along with anyone and everything else on this planet. Laws should always be obeyed, but once one becomes an independent adult or a self-employed adult or parent, there are new rules which one can make, but one earns the right to do this, by acquiring self-discipline.

Civil offences in the home may include the following: not putting laundry in the washing basket, leaving dirty cups in the room, leaving clothing or personal items in the living areas, not cleaning the toilet, bath or bathroom, a messy kitchen, swearing or name calling, etc. The consequences of these civil offences are not called punishment, but rather community service, because the child offended towards the rest of the community in the home and should make some kind of retribution towards the community.

Even if you employ a housekeeper or gardener, it is recommended that children also take responsibility for some communal chores around the home such as picking up dog pooh, cleaning the pool, putting out the dustbin, sorting the washing, sweeping the veranda, etc as this would teach them to become responsible adults who care for the community and their environment.

Civil offences and community service may for example include:

Offence	Community service
Forgetting a dirty cup in the room	Washing dishes that night
Not putting laundry in the basket	Doing the laundry that week

Name calling or swearing	Apology and making that person's bed for a week
Not cleaning the bath	Cleaning the bathroom for a week
Leaving bread crumbs and dirty cutlery on the kitchen counter	Cleaning and mopping the kitchen for two days
Borrowing without permission	Tidying up the person's cupboard or room for two days.
Neglecting chores, such as dog pooh, swimming pool, dustbin, etc.	House cleaning on a Saturday including dusting, polishing, vacuuming etc. or cleaning up the garage.
Losing an item of clothing or cell phone	Paying for it from pocket money.

Criminal offences in the home, on the other hand are more serious and usually pertain to lying, endangering own or someone else's safety or lives, violent behaviour including rage and tantrums, etc. These offences are punished either by fines, or by being grounded, just as criminals are fined or sent to jail. Punishment must also fit the crime, for example:

Offence	Punishment
Not alerting parents to your whereabouts	Cell phone social use suspended for a full two weeks and grounded for the next weekend.
Lying	No cell phone use for two weeks.
Breaking a curfew	Grounded for a week, including weekend.
Hitting, spitting or assaulting someone.	Apology and paying a fine to that person and being grounded for two weeks.

Breaking anything – including own possession deliberately	Replacing that item out of pocket money and grounded
Not locking security gates	Grounded for a week.
Serious offences such as drinking, drugs or stealing	Extensive grounding, barring of cell phone, therapy and rehab and no pocket money.

There are only three reasons why people lie, namely 1) not to get into trouble, 2) to protect someone else and 3) to get someone else in trouble on purpose. Children often lie simply because they don't know what the punishment for an offence would be and they fear getting into trouble. This is usually a sign of inconsistent discipline and severe punishment by parents. Once a child knows exactly what the consequences of his/her behaviour will be, they will be more likely to avoid that behaviour, or to take the punishment.

Parents should instil integrity in their children. A person with integrity does not take other people's money or possessions, does not lie, does not cheat in business or in private affairs, keeps promises, pay their taxes and licences, can admit when they have made a mistake and he/she can forgive. A person with integrity values the life force of people, animals, nature and possessions and treats these with respect. Children learn by example. If you want your child to grow up to become a law abiding, contributing, productive citizen and make adult life more easily for them, then set the example and tell them verbally about integrity.

It is recommended that both parents together make a list of civil and criminal offences first. This will be called the protocol. Then the children are invited to a round table family discussion and requested to come up with suggestions as to community service and punishments. Make sure they understand the principles of civil offences and community service versus serious crimes and punishment and explain the household functions like the state judicial system.

By asking them to come up with suggestions, the children will have a democratic input into the process. If a person feels he/she has made a democratic input, they are more likely to commit to the venture. (It is not now a case of: "When you live under my roof, you abide by my rules" - Now it is a case of: "We all live under this roof, so you have a say in the rules"). Parents of course have the right to veto suggestions, and just as the government has the right to make laws and determine punishment for serious crimes, parents have the right to set punishment for serious offences.

Differentiate between pre-school, primary school and teenagers. The younger the child, the less severe the service or punishment should be. The older children have more severe community services and punishment, but they also have more responsibility, more cell phone or computer privileges and freedom. Children should learn that freedom and responsibility go hand in hand. For instance, a grade 10 child may stay out until 10pm, but a grade 12 child until 12pm. Since young children do not go out, they cannot be grounded, but they can be sent to bed early or be barred from watching television instead.

The protocol of offences and related community services and punishments is then printed out. Each member of the household then signs this protocol as a gesture of commitment. A copy is then given to each member and one is placed for instance upon the fridge door, or behind the toilet. Parents must remember to sign this protocol too and if Mom or Dad offends by forgetting a dirty mug in the lounge then they must do the community service in good spirit. Adults are not above the law and must set a good example.

Once the protocol is singed, there is no bargaining about consequences unless there are true mitigating circumstances. Mitigating circumstances may reduce a consequence, but not set it aside and both parents must agree to it. (A cell phone's flat battery is not a mitigating circumstance for not alerting a parent to whereabouts. Children are not allowed to leave the premises with a flat cell phone battery – it is an offence. Parents can collect all cell phones at 21h00 and charge the phones. No teenager needs a cell phone after 21h00. They have to sleep. A stolen cell phone is mitigating for not being able to alert a parent, but the child should still face the consequences for not taking responsibility to ensure such an expensive item is safe.)

Children may close their bedroom doors and parents should knock and wait for an invite to enter, but children may not lock themselves in their rooms or bathrooms. Privacy is respected – there is no need to enforce it.

Having such a protocol would cut out on parents nagging children to do things. It's simple: You did something wrong or neglected to do something, you do the community service or take the punishment, as you committed yourself to the protocol. End of discussion.

Remember, children need at least three compliments for each criticism to build their self-esteem and confidence. Show appreciation for good behaviour and comment on it often.

It is also a good idea to reward children now and then for chores completed, but this is ad hoc and they should not expect a reward. As citizens we are all expected to keep our country clean and treat others with respect without reward. Treating them to a family outing over the weekend since everyone has completed their chores without complaining that week, will be a nice surprise. Allow them to vote as to where they would like to go. A drive to the country, tea, a visit to a museum or an expo, the theatre, horse riding excursion, etc are good examples and will promote quality family time. It would be great if each child can invite a friend along.

It is highly advisable that children receive pocket money. This not only teaches them to budget, appreciate the value of possessions and extend the gratification of their needs, but it also provides leverage for parents to fine or withdraw pocket money as punishment.

Children should pay all social expenses out of their pocket money. These include movie tickets, refreshments or meals when they go to malls, presents for friends, make-up, trinkets, costume jewelry, cd's, etc.

All items relevant to school projects, sports or trips, some social clothing and essential toiletries should be provided by parents.

The estimated amount should encompass spending money for one or two events per weekend for teenagers. This enables them to save up money for expensive "must haves". Children have a tendency to pay "cash for trash" and waste their money. Restricting pocket money, will eliminate this nasty habit, teach them to budget and consider twice before they just spend. They can also be encouraged to hold jumble sales, garage sales, etc to earn more money and become entrepreneurs. Parents can encourage savings by for instance contributing a quarter or half of each amount saved.

Children should learn to extend the gratification of their needs, for as adults we know we can't always just get what we want, and the world does not revolve around us. Children older than 16 can work over weekends to supplement income, eg at restaurants etc, but not during exam time. As a rule of thumb, it is advisable that children under 15 can go out one weekend night and older than 16 both weekend nights, provided they stick to curfews and the rules. Only one weekend night is advisable for both groups during exam time.

Many children have cell phones, but parents should restrict their cell phone budgets. They may add to it out of their pocket money. They should be punished if they consume the whole budget and do not have air time left for emergency calls to their parents. Their batteries should also be amply charged before they go out, so they have no excuse for not alerting parents to their whereabouts. It is the child's responsibility to check this and they should face the consequences if they neglect this. Although we should teach our children to respect other people's privacy, by respecting their privacy, but parents do have the right to monitor computers and cell phone for pornography and paedophiles and their rooms for drugs. Explain to the child why you do this, if you think you have reason. The police may also enter our premises with a search warrant if they suspect us of illegal conduct. Computers and cell phones used for such purposes can be confiscated.

Parents and children should not be friends on Facebook. It is however recommended that an aunt or some other adult keep an eye on the Facebook page of the child. Random checks on the friends on Facebook, in the company of the child – can be done.

If children sleep over or go out with friends for the evening, they should alert their parents if they change location, even if it is just from one restaurant to another in malls. Children and especially girls should not go to toilets alone in malls. Toilets are often located close to exits and parking lots and children can easily be abducted by grown men and kidnapped. They should always move in groups of three or more. Men's and ladies' toilets are also unfortunately located adjacent at the end of long corridors. Adult men can easily drag a young child into the men's toilets and rape him/her. Children should be made aware that alerting parents of whereabouts is a safety precaution that could prevent rape and murder and has nothing to do with not trusting them.

When divorced parents remarry then they should treat all the children in their home the same. All the children should adhere to the protocol of that home, regardless of the discipline in their other home. It would be excellent if divorced parents could agree with their ex-partners on the same protocol and this should be included in the legal parenting plan. If a child is grounded for a month due to a serious misconduct, then the divorced ex-parent should maintain this grounding even if the child is visiting that weekend. Spiting the other parent by allowing the child to go to a party is not beneficial for the child, for it teaches the child to manipulate and cheat.

The sooner a protocol for desired behaviour is administered in the home, the better, but it is never too late to implement one.

Good luck, enjoy the benefits of your desired behaviour protocol and watch your children to grow up into mature, law-abiding, productive adults.

© Dr Micki Pistorius

Terms and Conditions, Indemnity and Disclaimer

Copyright as well as intellectual property rights of the website: www. Heroes-Warriors.com and the Book: Heroes, a Psychological insight into men's perceptions on relationships belong to Micki Pistorius 2015. The moral right of the author has been asserted. Micki Pistorius is a brand which may not be copied, used, imitated in any form including printed, social media, internet. The author retains the rights to all animations, illustrations, video's, visuals, intellectual property, website, Facebook pages, contents, title, television, film, documentaries, cd's and marketing products.

The following terms and conditions apply to the provision and reader's use of the content through the Heroes-Warriors.com website, including the reader registering as a login user, and buyer of the kindle version or hard copy of the book entitled Heroes – a Psychological insight into men's views on relationships.

1   About us

1.1   In these terms, references to "we" or "us" are to the author, copyright and intellectual property owner, Micki Pistorius;
1.2   In these terms the Website refers to Heroes-Warriors.com;
1.3   In these terms the Contents or the Book refer to Heroes – a psychological insight on men's perceptions on relationships;
1.4   In these terms "you" or "your" are references to you as reader, buyer or registered login user.

2   Copyright

2.1   You agree not to distribute all or any part of the Book to any other party, in any medium without prior written consent from the author Micki Pistorius.

2.2   Receiving a pdf copy does not entitle you to forward it to someone else.

2.3   You will not copy, reproduce, create derivative works of, distribute, transmit, broadcast, display, sell, license or otherwise exploit any content contained in the Book.

3   Internet

3.1   You agree that the posting of your comments or contributions to the heroes-warriors Facebook page is subject to the editing and sole discretion of the author Micki Pistorius and we are under no obligation to post them on the website.

3.2   You agree that all your comments and contributions posted to the Facebook page messenger, may be open for the public to read and other users to comment on, either on Facebook or the website.

3.3   You agree that any part of your comment may be used as a Review on the Website or Facebook page.

4   Links

4.1   Any links to websites and those linked sites may contain content or offer products and /or services for sale.

4.2   We do not author, edit, control or monitor Linked Sites and you agree that we have no responsibility for the accuracy or availability of information provided by Linked Sites.

4.3   We will not be liable for any transactions conducted by you with third parties through any Linked Site or for any liability arising from any representations or information provided by such Linked Sites.

5   Disclaimer and Indemnity

5.1   You agree that the content of the Website, Facebook page and the Book is not intended as a replacement for one-on-one therapeutic relationship with a registered health care professional.

5.2   You agree that at no time should the contents be interpreted or construed as personal therapy, legal advice or medical advice.

5.3   You agree that no personal correspondence will be entered into by the author Micki Pistorius and under no circumstances will the author provide personal therapeutic consultations to subscribers through this media.

5.4   You agree that you will not make any inferences as to the identity of the persons behind the case studies discussed in the Book and that all effort has been made to protect the identities of such persons.

5.5   You agree we provide the content of the Website and the Book in good faith but give no warranty or representation that the content is complete or up to date or that it will meet your requirements, nor that the Website or the Book does not infringe the rights of any third party.

5.6   You agree that your use of the Website and the Book is entirely at your own risk.

5.7   You agree that you indemnify and keep us fully indemnified from and against all actions, claims, demands, costs, expenses, liabilities, loss, damage or any other monetary relief brought, made or awarded against or incurred by us resulting (directly or indirectly) from:

Your submitting content to the Facebook page;

Your access to the Website and reading / interpretation of the Book;

Any negligent act or omission, deliberate default or breach of the terms and conditions on your part.

8   Changes to the Website and the Book

8.1   We may update or amend these Terms from time to time to comply with the law or to meet our changing business requirements, without notice to you. Any updates or amendments will be posted on the Website.

8.2   By continuing to use the Website and the Book, you agree to be bound by the terms of these updates and amendments.

www.ingramcontent.com/pod-product-compliance
Lightning Source LLC
Chambersburg PA
CBHW072042280526
45788CB00006B/2151